Turkey's State Crisis

Contemporary Issues in the Middle East
Mehran Kamrava, *Series Editor*

Select Titles in Contemporary Issues in the Middle East

Democracy and the Nature of American Influence in Iran, 1941–1979
David R. Collier

Generations of Dissent: Intellectuals, Cultural Production, and the State in the Middle East and North Africa
Alexa Firat and R. Shareah Taleghani, eds.

The Lost Orchard: The Palestinian-Arab Citrus Industry, 1850–1950
Mustafa Kabha and Nahum Karlinsky

Making the New Middle East: Politics, Culture, and Human Rights
Valerie J. Hoffman, ed.

Ottoman Children and Youth during World War I
Nazan Maksudyan

Political Muslims: Understanding Youth Resistance in a Global Context
Tahir Abbas and Sadek Hamid, eds.

Readings in Syrian Prison Literature: The Poetics of Human Rights
R. Shareah Taleghani

Understanding Hezbollah: The Hegemony of Resistance
Abed T. Kanaaneh

For a full list of titles in this series, visit https://press.syr.edu/supressbook-series/contemporary-issues-in-the-middle-east/.

Turkey's State Crisis

Institutions, Reform, and Conflict

Bülent Aras

Syracuse University Press

Syracuse, New York 13244-5290

First Edition 2022

22 23 24 25 26 27 6 5 4 3 2 1

∞ The paper used in this publication meets the minimum requirements of the American National Standard for Information Sciences—Permanence of Paper for Printed Library Materials, ANSI Z39.48-1992.

For a listing of books published and distributed by Syracuse University Press, visit https://press.syr.edu.

ISBN: 978-0-8156-3748-6 (hardcover)
978-0-8156-3734-9 (paperback)
978-0-8156-5535-0 (e-book)

Library of Congress Control Number: 2021936801

Manufactured in the United States of America

To Asuman, Süheyl Enis, and Elif

Contents

Tables

Acknowledgments

This book is based on my research, experience, and observations on the foreign and security policy apparatus of the Turkish state over many years. Our projects on conflict resolution following the July 2016 coup attempt in Turkey at the Istanbul Policy Center (IPC) helped me put together my ideas into policy papers and articles, later making this book possible. I am deeply grateful to Pinar Akpinar for her leading role in these projects and her critical inputs to my research. I am also grateful to the IPC staff who worked with me over the years: Megan Gisclon, Cana Tülüş Türk, Meryem Kösehasanoğulları, Ayşe Köse Badur, Ozgül Kızıldağ, Elif Gencer and Emir Kırdan. I completed this book in 2020 when I was a visiting researcher at Rensselaer Polytechnic Institute in Troy, New York.

I had the privilege to be a student of Kemal Kirişçi and M. Nazif Shahrani, and to work with Fuat Keyman. They inspired many, including myself, to study Turkey, the Middle East, and beyond. I had the opportunity to work with Ahmet Davutoğlu, Hakan Fidan, and Ibrahim Kalın and owe them a great deal for sharing their perspectives and experiences. I am also indebted to my colleagues at the Ministry of Foreign Affairs, with whom I shared four years (2009–13) of tireless and dedicated work at a very critical period for Turkey. I would like to thank Vassilis K. Fouskas, Bülent Gökay, and Emirhan Yorulmazlar, who have been my greatest friends and supporters in my studies through all these years.

There are far too many colleagues and friends to thank for their help and advice along the way of writing this book: Jose Holguin-Veras, Şaban Kardaş, Gürsel Dönmez, Mahir Ünal, Talip Küçükcan, Murat Yeşiltaş, Ferhat Pirinççi, Christian Ostermann, Max Hoffman, Michael Werz, Senem Aydın Düzgit, Ersin Kalaycıoğlu, Cemil Aydın, Özge Genç, Şule

Toktaş, Metin Gürcan, Bahri Yılmaz, Korel Göymen, Mustafa Akyol, Emad Shahin, Richard Falk, Hilal Elver, Azmi Bishara, Ebtesam al-Ketbi, Paul Salem, Ayşe Kadıoğlu, Meltem Müftüler, Hasan Selçuk, Altay Atlı, and Aftab Kamal Pasha. I would also like to thank Mehran Kamrava for the encouragement to submit this book to Syracuse University Press and Margaret A. Solic, acquisitions editor, for her help preparing the manuscript, and anonymous readers for their comments on an earlier draft.

Two of my published articles are incorporated into this book: "State, Institutions, and Reform in Turkey after July 15," *New Perspectives on Turkey* 59 (2018), and "Crisis and Change in Turkish Foreign Policy after July 15," *Alternatives: Global, Local, Political* 44, no. 1 (2019). Most of the interviews with bureaucrats, politicians, and journalists are unattributed. However, they deserve special thanks for their time and courage to share their ideas in this difficult period of change and transformation in Turkey. I would also like to thank my colleagues at the Sasakawa Foundation, Brookings Institution, Center for American Progress, Georgetown University at Doha, University of Malta, National University of Singapore, Jawaharlal Nehru University, Wilson Center, Chicago Council on Global Affairs, Chinese Academy of Sciences, Korea Institute for International Economic Policy, Russian Academy of Sciences, and Keele University for providing me with venues to discuss some of my ideas presented in this book.

My special thanks go to my family: my wife, Asuman; our daughter, Elif; and our son, Süheyl Enis. They were exposed to my ideas more than ever as we were practicing social distancing and self-isolation against the COVID-19 pandemic in the final preparation phase of this book. I dedicate this book to them. I alone am responsible for any mistakes in fact or judgment in it.

Niskayuna, New York, April 2020

Turkey's State Crisis

Introduction

Recurrent State Crisis

What accounts for the regression of Turkey's stature from a model country to one riddled with state crisis, authoritarianism, and conflict? With Turkey's much-appraised role as a democratic and prosperous Muslim country in decline over the last decade, the recent focus on Turkey has magnified the schisms of democracy versus authoritarianism, secularism versus political Islam, and rule of law versus dictatorship. Yet, the unique case of Turkey has also reflected a prevailing but largely disregarded dynamic: that of reform versus conflict. Turkey has backtracked on its reform agenda, waived its role in conflict resolution at home and abroad, and consequently lost its ability to project soft power in its neighborhood.

Despite the discussion on Turkey's democratic or institutional backsliding, the underlying causes of this regression have not been comprehensively analyzed. This book aims to decipher the historical, political, and geopolitical background of the unwinding of Turkey's reform process and to analyze the resultant state crisis and conflictual foreign and security policy. Trying to offset the hegemonic power of the military-civilian bureaucracy, the governing Justice and Development Party (AKP) consolidated its alliance with certain segments of liberal and secular groups, as well as the Gülenists, following the Constitutional Court's unsuccessful attempt to close the AKP in 2008. This haphazard attempt to fill in—or more precisely, crowd out—the gargantuan role of the bureaucracy in the Turkish state system created a void that has been aggravated by growing polarization, zero-sum logic, and political infighting across Turkey in the later period of AKP rule (2010–20).

Overall this setting has vindicated the urgency of reform. A closer inspection of Turkey's public administration and foreign policy highlights the failure of the reform agenda after the virtual stall in Turkey's European Union (EU) accession process and the subsequent vicious cycle of conflict reproduction. The July 15, 2016, coup attempt was a tipping point in the case for political reform, as the recurring inability to transform and redefine the political arena saw the erosion of state authority, disorganization of the bureaucratic apparatus, and failure to introduce a reconciliatory approach to politics.

The government's post–July 15 reform designs were largely defined by haphazard attempts to consolidate the AKP's hegemonic electoral power, which lacked the tenets of a merit-based bureaucratic order and institutional state reform. The so-called Turkish-type presidential system, largely built on the need to accommodate President Recep Tayyip Erdoğan's quest for omnipotent executive rule, unbound the separation of powers and weakened rule of law. In addition to his electoral victories, Erdoğan defeated what he calls bureaucratic tutelage in the context of his party, namely controlling judiciary and military. Following the extraordinary powers of the emergency rule after the 2016 failed coup, Erdoğan was given new presidential authority, and he was virtually unchallenged. The end result since the April 2017 constitutional referendum has not been an idealized managerial executive system, but rather a dysfunctional state system with undefined and untested roles for state organs and the bureaucracy, which has been further aggravated by the AKP's general tendency to suffocate institutional policy making.

Against this background the recurrence of the Turkish state's hegemonic and coercive approach to conflict resolution has sidelined the political opposition as well as civil society. The political, systemic, security, and identity crises have together undermined Turkish foreign policy's traditional role in paving the way for domestic reform. Rather, foreign policy entanglements have fed into Turkey's insecurities and led to the perpetuation of conflictual policies in the domestic realm and in Turkey's relations with its neighbors. A reassessment of Turkey's political transition supports the argument that Turkey must either double down on reform or become further embroiled in conflict in both the domestic and external arenas. Against this backdrop the book portrays a feasible way to reinstate a constructive reform process and offers policy guidelines toward state reform and recalibration in foreign policy.

The purpose of this book is to delineate the background of the state crisis in Turkey. The erosion of its founding myths notwithstanding, the Turkish state has been in crisis mode since the end of the Cold War. Unable to adapt to the challenges of the era, with the need to respond to ethnic and multicultural political demands for reform, the Turkish state has resisted change and stuck to its ideational roots stemming from the 1930s. In essence the ideals of homogeneity and monolithic understanding of national unity have contradicted the multicultural roots of the country. As a result Turkey has faced a deep identity crisis due to growing political, security, and geopolitical challenges. The politics of secularism and the straitjacket of Turkish nationalism have clashed with the identity politics of Islamism and Kurdish nationalism. NATO membership has failed to protect Turkish interests from Iraq to Bosnia and in the context of the secessionism of the Kurdistan Workers' Party (PKK).

The Western geopolitical identity demanded normative conformity but disregarded the Turkish quest for security cover. The resultant state crisis paved the way for the rise of the AKP in the 2002 elections, which saw the collapse of all mainstream parties save the Republican People's Party (CHP). The AKP's secret in holding on to power was its proven record of owning the reform process in the 2000s, from Turkey's EU accession to the Islamic, Kurdish, Cypriot, and Armenian questions in Turkish politics. The policy of open-minded reform also led to a constructive foreign policy agenda, which beefed up the case for domestic reform.

In any case, the reformists in Turkey had to stand up against the rejectionists among the state cadres. The bureaucracy—which had played a flag-bearer role in Turkish modernization—had been skeptical about the prospects of readjusting the founding ethos of the Turkish Republic. Even if its modernist propensities allowed for further Westernization, the perceived twin threats of Islamism and Kurdish nationalism defied any idea of reform among the state elites. The secular and nationalist political parties also carried a similar distaste for what they considered destabilizing reform.

Turkey's State Crisis studies the relationship between political elites and the bureaucracy, with a close focus on institutions as agents of performance and delivery in the provision of public policy. It investigates the state crisis from several perspectives: the political elites' attempt to change the administrative system to create a performance-oriented one; the bureaucracy's response, concerns, and resistance to change; the state's conflict resolution capacity; and the transformation of foreign and security policy. All in all this book is an attempt to present a comprehensive picture of state crisis in Turkey in reference to structural elements of recurring crises; it provides guidance for reforms to break the vicious cycles of political polarization, rising authoritarianism, and weak state institutions.

The book's general argument revolves around the thesis that the AKP government's shift to power consolidation and later inability to sustain the reform process derailed its initial case for conflict resolution at home and abroad, as well as its performance in the delivery of public services. Despite initial ownership, the AKP leadership failed to uphold its commitment to consensual reform. In the background the political rivalry between the government and bureaucracy–cum–secular establishment engendered a climate of political polarization and deinstitutionalization. Thus, particularly in the aftermath of the coup attempt in July 2016, the AKP fell into the trap of marginalizing the opposition and defying even moderate calls for consensual reform in the context of its supposedly invincible electoral power.

To substantiate this argument the book delves into the historical, political, and geopolitical background of the state crisis. It reflects on the author's academic studies and experience of working within the Turkish state apparatus. It also includes a wide array of interviews with policy makers and state elites. With a blend of academics' and practitioners' perspectives, the book addresses the key questions of bureaucratic reform; the state-society relationship; the role of the opposition and civil society in the reform process; the relationship between state capacity and conflict resolution; the Turkish state's traditional methodology of conflict resolution and its effects on conflict reproduction; foreign policy's role in setting the stage for reform or aversion to reform; the correlation between growing insecurities abroad and the domestic reform agenda; the reverberant effects of political, systemic, security, and identity crises on state crisis and foreign policy; and the geopolitical causes of Turkey's disassociation from a reform agenda and its increasing association with hard-power choices.

The book begins by addressing the background of the state crisis in Turkey. The erosion of state capacity due mainly to bureaucratic decay and political crises has underlined the insurmountable need for state reform. Unable to steer a feasible and functional route to reform in the context of a setting of polarized political rivalry, the state apparatus failed to live up to its traditional role as the ultimate decision maker in conflict resolution. In the foreign and security policy arena, the growing challenges not only suffocated the domestic reform agenda but also thrust Turkey into a vicious cycle of conflict reproduction and its resultant insecure and insular worldview. Against this backdrop the book magnifies the present challenges of state reform, paying close attention to institutional dynamics. It concludes with proposals for a feasible way to reinstate a constructive reform process.

1

Turkey's Political Crisis

Turkey has faced recurrent political crises since early Turkish modernization. The transition from what Machiavelli called "the monarchy of the Turk"[1] to constitutional monarchy and later republicanism has been defined by continuous conflict between the center and the periphery.[2] Following this historical dichotomy, the political transition, which has gained pace particularly since 2010, turned into a competitive, even destructive, process that has also become the underlying dynamic of Turkey's contemporary political crises.

The present Turkish political crisis under the Justice and Development Party (Adalet ve Kalkınma Partisi, AKP) has elevated the crisis to a whole new level. While Turkey saw its first-ever civilian electoral transition to a new constitutional order through the referendum on presidential rule on April 16, 2017, both the means and ends through which the ruling party achieved this transition have been far from democratic. Rather, the ruling party used electoral processes to minimize checks and balances in the system and sought to gain hegemony over the political system. The idea of democratic political transition slowly evaporated as the ruling party continuously overstepped the legal limits on political power. Thus the elected president rose to a unique position, with overwhelming control over the executive, legislative, and judicial branches of government. The transformation from a parliamentary system to presidential rule also turned the parliament, the constituent organ of the secular Republican regime, into a virtual nonplayer in the political system.

In this ever-present dichotomy of center versus periphery, the main political opposition, the Republican People's Party (Cumhuriyet Halk Partisi, CHP) has distanced itself from the statist discourse cherishing the founding premises of the strong state. Instead, it has rediscovered a cause célèbre for standing against the government's misuse of state power against the people. As a result, while the presidential system foresaw a popular rule that would accommodate the liberalizing calls of the opposition, the opposition seems to have found a new role to stand against the hegemonic power of the most powerful president.

While the quality of Turkish democracy has been dubious at best, the call for further democratization and liberalization was what essentially brought the AKP to power in 2002. The country's promotion of democratic rule, rule of law, and a market economy resulted in large-scale support from the peripheral segments of the Turkish electorate. It also enabled the emergence of a coalition of AKP liberal elites to set the stage for Turkish association with the (European Union) EU in the post–September 11 and post-Helsinki era.[3] After almost two decades of AKP rule, most scholars conclude that the AKP rose to power with the prospect of democratizing Turkey and liberalizing the political system by extending civil rights. The crux of the matter, then, is what explains the divergence from this early call for democratization and liberalization toward authoritarianism, centralization of state power, and the rebuke of nonmajoritarian interests? In essence, there has been a clash between the call for political reform and state interests.

In the academic literature, explanations of political crisis vary from hegemonic party rule to legal authoritarianism and from electoral effectiveness to transformation under state capitalism. The political crisis is what the political and state actors made of it in the past two decades, with their roots in earlier periods. In this sense, the roots of Turkish authoritarianism are by no means an exclusively current issue and entail a closer elaboration of the underlying forces defining it. Our analysis in this chapter will deal with the roots, causes, characteristics, and nature of the political crisis in the context of political and institutional reforms in Turkey.

The ruling cadre's use of state power is central to this argument. This chapter will deal with the following questions in order to shed light on the complex dynamics of the political crisis and the relevance of this crisis to the urgent call for state reform in Turkey: What is the balance between projecting infrastructural power and coercive power in governance? How do the ruling party and its leader manage the institutional setting in an environment of weak institutionalization? Is the political regime willing to open up space for rethinking, recalibrating, and restructuring itself, or would it defy alternative thinking as a threat to its stability and power projection? Does the political environment leave room for reformist thinking and politics? Is polarization the modus operandi of electoral competition in the country? How can political crisis be associated with state crisis vis-à-vis political change?

Tutelary Democracy to Hybrid Governance (2002–2010)

When the AKP came to power in the early 2000s, its ruling elite depicted themselves as the "powerless government" in the context of the so-called bureaucratic tutelage in Turkey. This perception was not far from reality if one evaluates the earlier relationship between the AKP and the core institutions of the state establishment, the military and judiciary, in this period. However, the AKP did not hesitate to continue instrumentalizing this perception of victimhood and social suffering as strategies for political action in Turkey, even once in power. The strong sense of victimhood is an important part of the party's hegemonic imagination, which "aims to expose how this reactionary mood profoundly depends on contradictory subjectification processes, which simultaneously involve mobilization of feelings of impotency, non-responsibility, self-pitying, and sublimation of power."[4]

The AKP's projected vulnerability also paved the way for the party's political alliances with frustrated secular segments of society, which saw the AKP as a new, potentially liberalizing actor in Turkish politics. Duygu Ersoy and Fahriye Üstüner underline that liberal intellectuals provided overt support for the AKP in the period between 2002 and 2010. They argued, "The main tool in attaining these positions was the idea of the powerless government, which was brought up to justify the misdeeds of the AKP."[5]

Desecuritization and Reform

The recurrent state crises in Turkey should be analyzed in the context of the backdrop of the never-ending power game between the military-judiciary bureaucracy and the political elite. Relations between these two groups are based on mistrust. According to Metin Heper, "From the 19th century onwards, the bureaucratic and military elites acted in the belief that they were solely responsible for maintaining order and modernizing their country."[6] Moreover, the bureaucratic and military elites' tendency to frame political issues as existential threats crowded out constructive public debate. At times public debate was restricted if the elites thought it threatened the secular character of the state. The mobilization of this perception through street protests had paradoxically thwarted public debate and brought further polarization. At other times Turkish intellectual life had been constrained by nationalist discourses that inhibited comprehensive discussion of minority and human rights.[7] In this power game the political elites occasionally became promoters of enemy and threat themes on various issues in an effort to build public and institutional support.

After 1999, when Turkey and the EU officially started membership talks, the scope and margins of national debate were extended to address securitized areas such as greater rights for individuals and ethnic groups within Turkey and traditional foreign policy questions such as Cyprus and the Kurdish and Armenian questions. Turkish affluence and growing self-confidence[8] in the international sphere also helped in expanding the space for debate. At the turn of the millennium, Turkey's major issue was the question of integrating Islam and Kurdish identity into Turkish politics. The AKP seemed to have normalized the perennial question of the compatibility of Islam and democracy and, as a result, aimed to assume a larger role in the Islamic world by setting a good example of their compatibility; this came to be known as the Turkish model.[9] The AKP turned itself into a majority governance-oriented party with mass appeal and large-scale public support. Despite occasional suspicions and misperceptions, the AKP embodied the transformation of Islam and politics not only in Turkey but also in the broader Islamic geography.

Before the 2000s the Turkish state was less accommodating on the Kurdish issue. Bureaucratic elites had long ignored and even attempted to deny the existence of the Kurdish question, insisting that the core of the problem was basically a regional development issue that certain groups hijacked to promote terrorism and separatism. Beyond this pretense, however, how the state treats its Kurdish population has become a benchmark for Turkish democratization both in domestic politics and international forums. Without curbing the security-oriented outlook on the Kurdish question, Turkish democracy has proven unable to develop a more inclusive and legitimate discourse vis-à-vis the Kurds and Turkish society in general.[10] Recep Tayyip Erdoğan has held a favorable view of integrating Kurds into mainstream Turkish politics, using Islamic thinking to equalize Turks and Kurds as Muslims. Among his entourage there have been prominent Kurdish figures who played critical roles in ensuring sustained Kurdish support for the AKP.[11] In 2005 Erdoğan crossed a critical threshold and acknowledged that "the state made mistakes about the Kurdish issue."[12] He has also repeatedly emphasized the Kurds' right to express their culture and identity. This proved to be a significant turning point in the historical question, given that simply speaking about Kurdish rights had previously been perceived as a threat to the state.

In the same period, Bülent Arınç, then speaker of the parliament, claimed that the Turkish parliament was completely excluded from the process of drafting Turkey's National Security Document and suggested that this was evidence of the power of a secret and antidemocratic structure.[13] Academics working on security issues also called for the "demythologyzing" of national security.[14] In this atmosphere journalists were emboldened to voice mounting criticism against the role of the National Security Council (MGK) and the classified status of the National Security Document. Even within the security establishment critical voices began to be heard. A retired senior officer from the Turkish National Intelligence Organization (MIT) wrote a newspaper article calling for change in Turkey's traditional stance on sensitive issues such as the headscarf, terrorism, and subidentities.[15] Some argued that the environment that emerged in the EU membership process was no longer receptive to the classical definition of national security.[16] Previously dramatized issues that were isolated from open and rational public debate began to be discussed within the realm of daily politics.[17]

Opposition to state policies by civil society groups began to be more and more tolerated, and this eventually led to more open debates on formerly securitized domestic and foreign policy issues. As a more concrete example, in December 2006 members of the foreign policy program of the

Turkish Economic and Social Studies Foundation (TESEV) paid a visit to Armenia to work toward the normalization of relations between the two countries.[18] Such openings began to introduce new perceptions and attitudes toward Turkey's neighborhood and change in foreign policy thinking. Likewise, another civil society organization, the Turkish Industry and Business Association (TÜSİAD), published a report on democratization in which it suggested that the Kurdish language should be taught in state schools as an elective course. Although nationalist circles lambasted this report, there was an open and fruitful national discussion on the issues raised in it. Obviously not all civil society organizations supported these moves. There were also newly emerging civil society organizations that defined themselves as secular, nationalist (*ulusalcı*), and Kemalist, and that attempted to draw particular domestic and foreign policy issues into the realm of national security in ways similar to those adopted by the Turkish military early on.

Other reforms at the domestic level as part of the EU membership process included shifting the balance of power within the (MGK) in favor of civilian members, appointing a civilian secretary-general for the MGK, removing military representatives from the Council of Higher Education and the Radio and Television High Council, and bringing the Turkish armed forces under the judicial control of the Court of Auditors. TÜSİAD's democratization report proposed that the chief of the General Staff should work under the defense ministry rather than under the office of the prime minister.[19] The weakening of the military's influence on foreign policy making was exemplified by the relatively silent position of the military establishment on certain foreign policy developments, such as the military's lesser role in the EU membership talks and the Turkish parliament's refusal to support the US-led coalition in Iraq.

Securitization and Survival

Changes in this securitized thinking culminated in mass demonstrations against the AKP government in April 2007. As the AKP sought reelection for the second time, the secular military establishment saw itself under threat from perceived Islamization and the dissolution of the state order.

These protests were organized by secular, Kemalist, and nationalist civil society organizations that pursued militant activism throughout this period. Although such organizations were both vocal and visible in the run-up to the July 2007 elections, the political party that is most often associated with this growing distaste with AKP policies, the CHP, was able to secure only 21 percent of the votes in the elections. The AKP's high share of votes can be seen as an indicator of the fragmented nature of Turkish society. Despite the accusations from mainstream political actors and public opinion that the AKP had a hidden Islamist agenda and was threatening the unity of the nation by granting rights to minorities and opening the Pandora's box on national security issues, the government still managed to secure broad public support.

The AKP and the Gülenists, followers of enigmatic cleric Fethullah Gülen, chose to collaborate in this insecure political environment despite their conflicting backgrounds, fluctuating relations, and divergent approaches to Islam and politics in Turkey. The apathy and distance between the two parties was already present when the AKP came to power. The Gülenists did not want to be associated with any form of political Islam, and the AKP wanted to keep the Gülenists at arm's length due to the secular regime's unwavering opposition to the group, which was believed to keep a hidden agenda of regime change beyond its purported business and community activities.[20] The AKP government's presence in the MGK meetings could not change the state's overall rejection of the Gülenists, particularly by the military elite, in the early years of AKP rule.

AKP-Gülenist relations turned into a tactical partnership under the imperatives of surviving in a zero-sum political environment. Shared concerns, primarily the fear of military and judicial power in Turkey, more concretely paved the way for this alliance. Both had been hit by the hegemonic power of the military-judiciary bureaucracy before and had joined forces to eliminate future threats. This marriage of convenience later spared the Gülenists from parliamentary motions and MGK decrees and enabled the AKP to sustain its political role through the EU membership track in the transitional period. However, the Gülenists' emphasis on EU membership in this period was undoubtedly beyond an innate call for further democracy. Rather, it was shaped by the expectation that the EU process could ward off what they called tutelary intervention and open up more space for civil society in the public sphere. The Gülenists' support for EU membership was reinforced after the EU-led change in the Counterterrorism Law in 2006, which resulted in Gülen's acquittal before he could be convicted for threatening the basis of the secular regime.

The AKP survived two major crises in this period. First, the prospect of replacement of a secular-Kemalist president, Ahmet Necdet Sezer, by an AKP-nominated president engendered serious fear and anxiety among the state elites, in particular within the military and judiciary. Commenting on the presidential election, Chief of the General Staff Yaşar Büyükanıt underscored, "I hope a president is chosen who is sincerely dedicated to the basic values of the Republic, the unitary structure of the state, and a secular and democratic state."[21] This statement indicated the military's will to reverse the probable course of the presidential elections, which were projected to result in an AKP victory. Accordingly the military issued an online memorandum on April 27, 2007, to block then–foreign minister Abdullah Gül's election as the next president of Turkey, largely because of his Islamist worldview and the fact that his wife was veiled. The AKP, despite serious second thoughts on whether it would serve its cause better to step back, moved to publicly counter the military's attempt to intervene. Failing to transcend judicial resistance to the presidential elections, the AKP called a snap election. Concurrently, Erdoğan put this disagreement between his party and the state elites—that is, electing the president by popular vote instead of the parliament—to a referendum in October 2007.

The second of these crises came when the chief prosecutor opened a court case to ban the AKP as a political party because of its antisecular activities and proclivities. The evidence for this argument relied largely on various statements from the AKP cadres and members of parliament, which mainly centered on the headscarf debates. The chief prosecutor's argument was approved by a majority of the members of the Constitutional Court, which concluded that the AKP had become "a focal point of antisecular political activities."[22] However, the six-to-five vote for closure fell short of the supermajority (three-fifths) needed to ban the AKP. Despite its greater victory, the AKP was still penalized and required to cut half of all treasury funds allocated to it for the elections.[23]

Following this decisive war of wills, the AKP and the Gülenists openly joined forces for an all-out offensive to break the military and judiciary's political power. First, they brought numerous active and retired military officials, including one former chief of staff, to dubious trials during the so-called Ergenekon and Sledgehammer (*Balyoz*) trials. These trials put hundreds of military and bureaucratic officials in prison and openly sought to minimize the military's role in Turkish politics. This partnership reached a new level when the Gülenists and the AKP attempted to change the composition of judicial bodies to their benefit through a constitutional referendum in 2010. These moves also received support from certain secular circles, which characterized their position as "incomplete but good" (*Yetmez ama evet*), referring to partial trust in democratization and reform under AKP rule.[24]

The AKP and the Gülenists appeared in utmost accord during this period. The AKP benefited from the Gülenists' human resource pool, while the latter took advantage of being more and more present in the top echelons of the bureaucracy through the appointment and promotion of their disciples, which also meant access to state resources and growing control of state institutions. As Hakkı Taş points out, "Claims of a Gülenist infiltration proliferated at the time, but the AKP opted for willful neglect."[25] A former AKP member of parliament claims that the Gülenists had many privileges in this period in comparison to other religious groups. The AKP governments not only were more than ready to accept the Gülenists' growing social, economic, and political power in Turkey, but also actively supported their outreach and schools outside the country.[26]

Hybrid Governance

The AKP preserved its founding principle of conservative democracy to a considerable extent in this period. The AKP employed characteristics of hybrid governance, which in this context implies a complex relationship between formal and informal actors that may or may not be harmonious. Hybrid governance "can be characterized by substitution, complementarity and incompatibility, with the latter leading to conflicts."[27] Turkey's version of hybrid governance has an imaginary negotiation table that provides recognition to informal actors and attempts to handle issues of statehood and national unity with them. The AKP benefited from these kinds of dealings with informal actors who brought their capabilities to help the AKP in government. In return these groups benefited from the state's symbolic and material resources. The AKP frequently needed this capacity for governance without resorting to coercive power in this period. The idea of a powerless government in the context of bureaucratic tutelage was enough to justify these relations and even secured support from groups who traditionally kept away from the AKP's worldview and certain policies.

Among the attempts to analyze this period, Nicole Pope argues that Erdoğan consolidated his power in order to later on establish "one-man rule."[28] M. Hakan Yavuz underlines the return of Islam in public space, relaxing state control of it, and the emergence of socially recognizable modes of Islam as hallmarks of the AKP era. He adds that the AKP reproduced the role of Islam in politics as an oppositional identity in the power struggles in contemporary Turkish politics.[29] According to Jenny White, Erdoğan attempted to move toward national unity by dominating social and political life in Turkey. This is a project the Kemalist cadres could not achieve since the early period of the republic.[30] The AKP's changing discourse and retooling in political practices, as Fatih Ceran argued, are the keys for understanding its position in Turkish politics.[31] Erdoğan overcame the political crises employing strategic and tactical retooling, which resulted in unprecedented control over the conservative-nationalist masses in Turkey. Although the AKP failed to meet broader expectations for liberalization and democratization, it was able to deliver administrative power and provide examples of good governance in social, political, and economic realms with a reformist approach and policies in this period.

Populism and Deinstitutionalization (2010–2020)

Erdoğan won the parliamentary elections in 2011 and presidential elections in 2014 and 2018, as well as the referendum for systemic change to an executive presidency in 2017. The need to secure a majority of voters and a preference for hegemonic rule not only forced Erdoğan to shatter

Table 1
AKP Political Alliances

Date	Alliances	Motives
2002–10	AKP-liberal groups	Democratization, liberalization, EU membership
2008–12	AKP-Gülenists	Eliminating tutelage, controlling military and judiciary
2018–	AKP-MHP-Ulusalcılar (ultranationalists)	Electoral alliance

his earlier choices for coalitions inside and beyond the AKP, but also further narrowed the party's inner cadres to a selective and, more important, loyalist group. This was also due to Erdoğan's fragile margin of electoral support, as he received only 51.7 and 52.9 percent of the voter share in the 2014 and 2018 presidential elections, respectively. Erdoğan formed a conservative-nationalist coalition, People's Alliance (Cumhur İttifakı), consisting of the AKP and the Nationalist Action Party (MHP) for the 2018 presidential elections. This two-party alliance proved capable of dominating the political system in Turkey.

Authoritarian Drift

After 2010 Erdoğan gained the ultimate upper hand, at which point he decided to challenge and tame the remains of the state apparatus on his own. Erdoğan had little faith in conciliatory politics, given his bitter experience with the bureaucracy and the failing Kurdish reconciliation process, particularly with the rise of Kurdish influence in postconflict Syria and Iraq. Rather than alleviating fragmentation and polarization, the dynamics of authoritarian rule maximized polarization and partisan politics in Turkey. Amid an ever-complex security environment, Erdoğan saw no choice but to lead his own front to electoral victory, which seemed to be the only way to secure his course to stabilize Turkey's economic development and ensure its continuation. The question is whether the resultant unique position of the AKP and President Erdoğan will result in the emergence of a political atmosphere conducive to reforms, unrealized so far. To put it another way, will President Erdoğan be willing to push for reforms in the aftermath of the political fights and elimination of rivals in the political sphere?

Berk Esen and Şebnem Gümüşçü assess the AKP's reform strategy from a similar angle and argue that Turkey has undergone two systemic political transformations under the rule of the AKP. These are the competitive authoritarian regime and tutelary democracy, the former made possible once the latter was phased out. Their evidence for this dual transformation is the two subsequent elections in 2015 and their paralyzing impact on the wider context of Turkish politics. They argue, "The fairness of elections is increasingly contested; civil liberties are systematically violated; and the playing field is highly skewed in favor of the incumbent AKP."[32] What remains at hand after these transformations is the consolidation of a "competitive authoritarian regime" in Turkey.

Ersin Kalaycıoğlu shares this perspective and questions the AKP's failure to form a coalition following the June 2015 general elections despite a tradition of successful coalition government formation in recent history. Political parties' uncompromising attitudes during the coalition-building attempts set the stage for the authoritarian shift in Turkey. He argues that terror attacks by the Kurdistan Workers' Party (PKK), along with the frustration of the nationalist masses, make it difficult for the CHP to enter a coalition that would include the pro-Kurdish party, the People's Democratic Party (HDP). On the government front, the ruling AKP followed President Erdoğan's assessment that a coalition government would result in the erosion of the AKP's power in due process. This failure brought Turkey back to the "polarizing politics of competitive authoritarianism under the hegemony of the one-party government of the AKP."[33]

Orçun Selçuk has developed a cross-regional perspective to compare political populism in Venezuela, Ecuador, and Turkey. He suggests that scholars should analyze three populist leaders—Erdoğan, Hugo Chávez, and Rafael Correa—through three interconnected "dimensions: an anti-establishment image, a plebiscitary understanding of democracy, and a Manichean worldview."[34] The analysis of the populist leaders in each country in this framework points out that "a strong leader positions himself against the traditional establishment, cultivates direct linkages between himself and his followers and polarizes the political environment into two opposing camps."[35] Michael Gunter boldly alleges that Erdoğan is impervious to the destruction of the institutional setting of the republic in his drive to establish an authoritarian regime in Turkey. Thus whoever opposes his methods would be easily classified as an enemy of the state in the aftermath of the failed coup in 2016. Since then Erdoğan has moved to eliminate all potential rivals and has created an environment of fear to control others. Gunter, therefore, finds the situation in Turkey similar to the early period of the Cultural Revolution in China.[36]

Karabekir Akkoyunlu and Kerem Öktem offer a more nuanced explanation by focusing on how existential insecurity within ruling cadres played a role in accelerating Turkey's transformation into an authoritarian regime. Ever-growing uncertainties and Erdoğan's search for constitutional regime change created a strong sense of insecurity that left him no choice but to seize an authoritarian hold on power.[37] Necati Polat identifies the AKP's push for regime change as "mimetic, imitative, [and] modelled on the other."[38] Regime change, according to the AKP, meant an end to the duality between the state and the government in Turkish politics. Polat explains that while the AKP respects state-government duality as an imitative form of a desired model, the search for the replacement of it is "predicated on a primordial form of violent rivalry."[39]

To manage a smooth transition from uncertainty to governance, the AKP's real challenge was to shape the leadership of the country so as to best serve the interests of Turkey in the aftermath of the November 2015 elections. There was growing opposition in Turkey and abroad to the authority of a single, dominant leader; this would not stabilize or stimulate economic growth, ensure diplomatic influence, or achieve political progress in an unchecked presidential system. In comparison, objections to a hegemonic party operating in a parliamentary system were far less reactive because it was thought that the relevant checks and balances were entrenched in the constitutional order. Political actors trusted that the second model could diminish toxic polarization, counter the allegations of authoritarianism, and address the most pressing problems at home and in the region.

Stemming the tide of increasing polarization and fragmentation in Turkish politics depended on the AKP leadership realizing that its electoral success in the repeated November 2015 elections was a mere last chance for fence-mending to stabilize the political order. However, in the aftermath of the elections, the AKP missed the opportunity to seek common ground and end the cycle of conflict. Rather, Erdoğan moved to eliminate even the pretense of opposition inside the AKP and committed himself to transforming what had been a largely ceremonial presidency into a dominant political position. In addition to then–prime minister Ahmet Davutoğlu, Erdoğan effectively sidelined former president Gül, the only other possible rival in the AKP ranks at that time. In due course these kinds of bold moves resulted in internal divisions in Erdoğan's political camp, with potential opposition initiatives on the horizon. Two parties, the Future Party (Gelecek Partisi) and Democracy and Progress Party (Demokrasi ve Atılım Partisi), have already been established, in December 2019 and March 2020, respectively, under the leadership of two prominent figures from Erdoğan's political ranks, former prime minister Davutoğlu and former deputy prime minister Ali Babacan.

In this political atmosphere there is no option for power sharing or delegating power in the new mindset of the government. Akkoyunlu and Öktem remind us of the roots of insecurity under former Kemalist tutelage while focusing on the escalation of insecurity under the AKP's Islamist project of transforming the regime.[40] Employing René Girard's anthropological insights, Polat argues that the AKP's shift from a reformist actor with democratic credentials to an authoritarian political figure is a reflection of the desire to destroy the other.[41] This Islamist project of domination resulted in intra- and inter-elite power struggles in state and politics. The stakes and associated risks in the domestic landscape were raised to an unprecedented level amid an environment of vicious political rivalries at home and growing fluidity in the neighborhood, particularly after the Arab Spring.[42]

Selçuk uses examples from the cases of Venezuela and Ecuador to draw parallels with the postcoup political environment in Turkey. He suggests that purges and the repudiation of the opposition are commonly used policies of populist regimes in these cases.[43] Emre Turkut underlines that the postcoup state of emergency provided wide-ranging powers to state authorities and a broad interpretation of counterterrorism measures imposed at the national level. The emergency decrees, in this sense, targeted not only coup plotters but also others who were thought to pose a threat to national security. Turkut emphasizes that Turkish authorities have a legitimate right to declare a state of emergency following an attempt to remove the elected government by force. However, he adds, "It may prove difficult indeed to establish the necessity and the proportionality of those far-reaching emergency measures that were imposed."[44]

Limits of Governance: The Kurdish Problem

What kind of an impact do all these dynamics and the emerging political atmosphere have on the governance capacity of the AKP? The populist and authoritarian shifts have varying impacts on governance in different cases; however, the issue of the Kurdish peace process is an exemplary case to observe the AKP's administrative pattern in transforming the political system. The peace process relied on negotiation, public deliberation, and democratization as possible steps toward peace. The negotiations between the Turkish state and the PKK, led by Erdoğan through Intelligence Chief Hakan Fidan and jailed PKK leader Abdullah Öcalan, constituted the backbone of the process. This high-level involvement demonstrated the strength of the political will on both sides. Public deliberation aimed to mobilize support and create societal ownership through transparent channels of communication and information. The Wise People Commission, which consisted of prominent journalists, academics, writers, unionists, businesspeople, and celebrities, informed people all across Turkey of visits and meetings on the peace process.

In a speech in the Kurdish-populated city of Batman in March 2014, Erdoğan declared, "The solution process was welcomed across Turkey and we, the AK Party government, are committed to it; we will proceed whatever the cost."[45] Öcalan was similarly committed. At the beginning of the process, in his Newroz messages in 2013 and in 2014, he announced, "The time of weapons is over; the time of politics has begun."[46] According to a

TÜSİAD report, the peace process would generate, on average, 1 percent of additional economic growth—that is, a value-added contribution of approximately US$8 billion for the region's economy, with further payoff for Turkey's general economic growth.[47] Numan Kurtulmuş, then–deputy chair for economic affairs of the AKP, cited another report asserting that the Kurdish problem had led to annual losses of 0.5 percent over the previous twenty-eight years.[48] A successfully implemented Kurdish peace process would have empowered Turkey by heightening its soft-power leverage in the region, enabling it to reap economic benefits and contribute to peace and stability.

The AKP made considerable progress in dealing with the Kurdish problem in Turkey, from increasing cultural and language rights for Kurds to negotiating with the PKK. According to Burak Bilgehan Özpek, the AKP's interaction with the PKK followed the institutional template of earlier strategies to gain the upper hand in political competition in Turkey. The AKP preferred negotiation rather than coercion in dealing with the Kurdish question. Özpek posits, "The AKP government regarded the peace process as an opportunity to avert the pressure and criticisms of domestic opposition and bolster its position in the political system."[49] Erdoğan's statement that he needed four hundred lawmakers to continue the peace process exemplifies his tactical use of the Kurdish problem in the June 2015 parliamentary elections.[50]

Contrary to expectations, the pro-Kurdish HDP gained visibility and momentum in the June 2015 elections and came to be represented in parliament despite the 10 percent threshold, which resulted in the AKP's loss of single party rule in the parliament and ended the peace process in the elections' aftermath. Regional security challenges and the ongoing political infighting with the Gülenists—who were declared a terrorist organization by the National Security Council in May 2014, having been designated as the FETÖ (Fethullahist Terror Organization) after their attempt to overthrow Erdoğan in the December 17–25, 2013, leaks—together with political constraints on systemic change not only narrowed the room for governance but also hinted at a return to the coercive measures used against dissident and minority groups in the 1990s.

Islam in Politics

Throughout its reign the AKP has used religion to keep the long-standing grievances of Islamic segments of society alive and has presented itself as the sole protector of their grievances and aspirations in the public sphere. The issue of the headscarf constituted a central place in the debate on secularism and Islam, which helped the AKP become both the owner of the Islamic cause and the leader of human rights advocacy in Turkey. After the ban on the headscarf was lifted, the debate on the role of Islam in daily life and politics did not end. Ahmet Erdi Öztürk argues that relations between Islam, the state, and Islamic groups directly affected the shift toward authoritarianism in Turkey. These interactions resulted in a new reasoning behind state-religion dynamics, and this new logic placed Erdoğan in a position of "somewhat supreme leader" in his dealings with Islamic groups in Turkey and Islamic causes abroad.[51]

Syaza Farhana Mohamad Shukri and Ishtiaq Hossain underline a correlation between the AKP's approach to Islam, which fluctuated in popularity throughout the years, and the changing political environment. The AKP refrained from defining itself as an Islamist or Islamic party at the outset; however, its Islamic identity gained primacy in the AKP's discourse, especially following the Arab revolts and the AKP's commitment to leading them. The 2011 elections were a tipping point for redefining the AKP's emphasis on Islamic identity; a content analysis examines the increased frequency of Islamist phrases appearing in party documents after 2011. The AKP's earlier approach to distancing itself from contentious religious issues shifted to a new strategy to utilize religion as a populist cause.[52]

Not surprisingly, differences between the AKP and the Gülenists resurfaced, and it became difficult to sustain the tactical alliance after 2010. The collision course was inevitable, but the Gülenists hijacked the AKP's electoral power in their cause to monopolize state power in line with a nonelectoral, in this sense tutelary, quest for regime change. Erdoğan's high profile in foreign policy and pragmatic line of recruiting new allies—for example, in the peace process—became irritants for the Gülenists.

Erdoğan seems to have been among the first to see the threat of the Gülenists and their growing demands for hegemonic control of state organs and the media and business sectors. He was unwilling to grant more concessions to the Gülenists, such as their demands before the 2011 elections to play kingmaker by appointing eighty to a hundred members of parliament within the AKP cadres and to further control the judiciary and security structures of the state. Gülen's public criticism of Turkey's position vis-à-vis the Gaza flotilla crisis, in which the flotilla was attacked by the Israeli Defense Forces in May 2010 (the *Mavi Marmara* incident), as an illegal adventure and a challenge to lawful authority[53] was a major volte-face, since it was the first time the Gülenists publicly questioned the AKP's foreign policy. The war of nerves reached a breaking point when a pro-Gülen public prosecutor called the chief of MIT, together with his predecessor and former deputy undersecretary, to testify before the court for pursuing secret talks with the PKK in February 2012. Erdoğan provided the highest level of protection to Fidan and former MIT staff and implicated the Gülenists in this attempt.

The conflict and political warfare between Erdoğan and the Gülenists quickly escalated after the Gülenist-led graft probe and arrests of AKP-related businesspeople, bureaucrats, and adult children of ministers on December 17 and 25, 2013, on charges of national and international corruption schemes, among other infractions. The rift over the planned closure of the breeding grounds of the Gülenist cadres, such as preparatory schools, and seizure of pro-Gülen media exemplified the unseen character and intensity of the political warfare between the AKP and the Gülenists, two prominent Islamic actors in Turkey. This rivalry ended in the decisive failed coup attempt on July 15, 2016, in which the Gülenists were again implicated. Immediately following the botched coup more than 150,000 public servants, including 17,000 military officials were sacked, and more than 40,000 people were arrested and imprisoned.

In order to make sense of the situation, Yavuz looks at the goals and strategies of secularism and Islamism in Turkish politics and argues that they represent two sides of the same coin in this context. The interaction between them shapes them and instigates the contest for the upper hand in political life. In his line of thought, new interpretations of Islam have been reproduced to consolidate power in contemporary Turkish politics.[54] There is a consensus among analysts that the AKP has an agenda for Islamization, and uses Islam as a tool for control of Turkish political life. According to Öztürk, there is no difference between how secularists and the AKP treat the relationship between Islam and the state, since both defend state control of Islam. The AKP's Islamic past and consciousness, and its later exclusion of the Gülenists have made it capable of dominating unofficial Islamic groups in the public domain. The situation is similar to earlier periods of secularist political control over various representations of Islam through coercion and resource allocation, but this time the force comes "only from the opposite direction."[55]

Conclusion

Assessing the evolving political crisis in Turkey, the Huntingtonian "third wave"[56] of democratization has proved inapplicable in the specific case of Turkey. This has been true in other countries' cases as well, as the wave of democratization in the 1990s was followed by a wave of authoritarian backlash.[57] Larry Diamond asserts that the decline of authoritarian regimes is over, and the trend of waning democracies stabilizes authoritarian rulers. He offers four reasons to believe that democratic recession is under way: the high number of failing democracies, problems in the application of democratic rules, authoritarian shifts in high-profile countries, and a lessening of interest in democracy promotion—for example, on the part of the United States.[58] In Turkey's neighboring geographies, the color revolutions in Eastern Europe and the so-called Arab Spring in the Middle East and North Africa indicated the difficulty of democratic transition, on the one hand, and authoritarian learning and resilience, on the other.[59] The rise of populism and authoritarianism at the global level did not create a favorable environment for the spread of democratic regimes when accompanied by authoritarian survival strategies in those countries.

Turkey's political crisis under AKP rule was created through the interactions between and among political and state elites over the past two decades, deepening and reproducing problems from earlier periods in

Turkish politics. The political crisis has both enabled and defined authoritarian rule under the ensuing systemic transition. This political atmosphere gave rise to polarization and deinstitutionalization, which have resulted in deadly blows to administrative power and strong barriers to good governance. Political polarization has divided the country into two camps, while deinstitutionalization has resulted in poor governance practices, which feed into the recurring state crisis in Turkey. It is not possible to differentiate between political crisis and state crisis as there is a complex web of interaction. The persistent political crisis under the presidential system is an indication that systemic change did not make the political atmosphere conducive to reform. The state crisis intensifies the urgent call for reform, but political polarization and deinstitutionalization make it nearly impossible for the willing parties to pursue a reform agenda.

2

State and Institutions in Turkey

The failed coup attempt on July 15, 2016, resurfaced the state crisis in Turkey, which was the driving force behind modernization efforts dating back to the early nineteenth century. Turkish modernization rested on an overarching motive to salvage the state, which above all meant modernization of the army and maintenance of the diplomatic balance of power. The resultant Weberian road map largely empowered the military and diplomatic bureaucracy, which in turn became the flag bearers of the modernization project. Absent organic links to society, the project failed to arrest the disintegration of the multiethnic Ottoman Empire and thus shaped the course of top-down nation building in the Republican era.

The modernization project failed to diffuse in the societal order, leaving the question of the integration of peripheral interests in the state structure. While the top-down state apparatus was largely left intact until the end of the Cold War, occasionally restored in the context of anomalies through bureaucratic interventions in the political order, in its aftermath the growing identity crises of the Republican polity gave way to the urgent need for integration of nationalist-conservative and ethnic-class concerns in the state structure. In theory this could have consolidated the state's power and strengthened the center through the inclusion of the periphery. Yet in practice it led to a continuous Kulturkampf between the

Parts of this chapter are reprinted with permission from Bülent Aras and Emirhan Yorulmazlar, "State, Institutions, and Reform in Turkey after July 15," *New Perspectives on Turkey* 59 (2018): 135–57. doi.org/10.1017/npt.2018.23. © *New Perspectives on Turkey* and Cambridge University Press.

secular-modern center and Islamic conservative-nationalist periphery, while leftist Kurdish and Alevi identities were generally pushed to the margins of Turkish politics.

The political will to reform set the stage for the bureaucratic center's resistance to change and the conservative periphery's predicament in struggling against the bureaucratic leviathan, particularly after what was called the February 28 process, in 1997. The end result of this process was loosening of the bureaucratic cadres' grip of the center, which amounted to the gradual erosion of bureaucratic power, rather than a paradigm shift toward the empowerment of civil society. While the bureaucratic "modernization" process proved unsustainable, the vacuum was filled by the hegemonic role of the governing political party, the Justice and Development Party (AKP), which first co-opted and then sought to eliminate the bureaucratic resistance with a broad-based coalition of the Gülenists, moderate Kurds, and liberal-secular Turks.

In return, particularly after the 2011 electoral victory and 2013 Gezi protests, the Gülenists, with their predominance in bureaucratic cadres after taking over the predominant role that had been held by the military-secular cadres following the decisive 2010 constitutional referendum and subsequent large-scale purges, fought back to delegitimize the AKP government both at home and abroad. In due course, the multiple failures in the management of the peace process between the state and the Kurds, and the Kurdistan Workers' Party's (PKK's) state-building ambitions in Syria and Iraq put Turkey back into a security-first outlook and undermined democratization efforts and relations with Western and regional countries. Simultaneously the liberal minority, advocating European Union (EU) integration through lobbying and intellectual power, lost touch with the AKP's increasingly nationalist-conservative agenda.

Against this murky background, July 15 was an attempt to overthrow the elected government, dissolve the parliament, and impose full control on the state apparatus. The putschists acted on the parochial legacy of Turkish politics: the principle that whoever controls the state authority projects a hegemonic hold on the Turkish political regime. Now that the Gülenist project to impose a syncretic and largely ambiguous pro-Western and Muslim identity on the Turkish state is over, the political arena has again become ripe for transformation, which the AKP under President Recep Tayyip Erdoğan maintains its claim to lead.

The structural capacity deficit and lack of institutionalization are the foremost problems for the Turkish state in averting such imposition of particularistic interests. Indeed, the coup attempt and the massive purges in its aftermath have brought the state to a breaking point. The state crisis has transpired in the middle of a political transition process whereby the ruling party has tried to justify change in the political system from parliamentary to presidential. In order to offset what has been dubbed bureaucratic tutelage, Erdoğan spearheaded a campaign to eliminate alternative levers of power, which would in the end neutralize the parliamentary and judicial checks over executive authority. The constitutional amendments also imply changes in the administrative order, with further political hold on bureaucratic cadres.

This chapter discusses the ways, means, and prospects for capacity development and institution building to overcome the state crisis in Turkey. What is the root cause of the problem of state crisis in Turkey? Does history tell us anything about the state crisis? What are the precedents of state reform in Turkey? What are the impediments to reforming the administrative structure in Turkey? Would system change in Turkish politics facilitate such a reform? How does state crisis make sense in the bureaucracy and among the political elites? What is the relevance of democracy to the problem of capacity and institutions? This chapter seeks answers to these questions.

State in Turkey

The recent literature on state capacity focuses on the ability to keep a state apparatus harmonious, to protect stability, and to manage the economy, and on the state's performance in doing so. States are categorized as strong or weak depending on their ability to deliver essential public goods, including security and welfare. This approach falls short of explaining the changing performance of a state in varying functions or in different times. In addition, it does not say much about the reasons some states are weak. Finally, the literature ignores the nuances between governance and state capacity.[1]

Turkey's state building followed the path of modern state formation, with the priorities of providing security, identity, and welfare to the citizenry. The Republican founding fathers pursued state-building efforts to render themselves as the undisputed authority within the new national borders and to obtain legitimacy vis-à-vis the international system. Their efforts were to some extent the continuation of earlier reform movements in the Ottoman era. Carter Findley points to the emergence of legal rationalism and a modern sense of statehood in the context of the traditional patrimonialism of the Ottoman system.[2] This worldview became a normative basis for government in the eyes of reformist cadres in the imperial state. Metin Heper supports this assumption and argues that this legal rationalism had been the widely shared perspective in an expanding and widening bureaucracy since the Tanzimat period.[3]

Exemplifying the complexity of the discussion, the idea of the state in Turkish history is almost identical to that of a capable state.[4] In this line of logic, the reason behind the dissolution of former states within the same geography has been the erosion of the state as a patrimonial provider. There were various motives for acquiring and protecting the strong state in former state formations. According to Osman Turan, the medieval Turks held an ideal of world domination that was intrinsic to their belief system and was perpetuated after Islamization, with the state acting as a defender of Islam in military and political terms.[5] Halil Inalcık explains the six-hundred-year reign of the Ottoman Empire through the state's strict adherence to the ideal of justice.[6] In this line of thought, born out of the classical worldview of the Empire, the state was strong when it performed the ability to provide justice and followed principles of Islamic and Sultanic law to that end. In contrast, the Republican choice was to build on the path of political centralization and mark the state as the first and last resort of modernization, with a broader objective to establish political and social control. For the Republican elites, a strong state was measured by the success of the modernization project in all aspects of life, from education to institution building, even if there had been disproportionate emphasis on security.[7]

The centralized state structure placed itself above political and civilian spheres and considered state institutions, including the judiciary and the bureaucracy, as its extension for transforming and modernizing society. This symbiotic model, which had early successes until the multiparty era, failed to adapt to the needs of democratic and popular rule. The result has been, at best, an uneasy coexistence of elected government and selected cadres of military-civilian bureaucracy. This dichotomy, in turn, set the stage for the presence of a modern state structure with deficits of performance and implementation and incomplete democratic consolidation. The Turkish case of government-bureaucracy relationships not only fell short of Weberian legal-rationalistic ideals of ensuring stability and bestowing predictability to the regime, but also undermined the popular quest for democratization—that is, representation—in large part because the bureaucracy had assigned itself the role of determining the contours of modernization. In any case, the latter's sui generis role was used for social control and to intervene on behalf of protecting the regime's founding principles, above all secularism and nationalism. The Turkish state has also shown a willingness to adapt its structure in conformity with foreign policy alignments—for example, multipartism in the wake of World War II and in the EU integration process after the Cold War—to adjust governance capabilities in order to ensure popular and international legitimacy.

The two qualities of this symbiotic model also gave rise to concurrent paradoxes of state power in Turkey. First is the Turkish state's lack of expertise and preparedness vis-à-vis societal crises. The confusion of the ruling elite in the face of social upheavals was one of the main reasons for an overall failure in conflict resolution in Turkey. This defect was epitomized not only in the broader Kurdish question, but also in smaller-scale local, sectoral, and environmental conflicts. Second, the popular government's quest for legitimacy vis-à-vis the bureaucracy boosted the urgency of developmentalism and capacity building. However, even if developmentalism aimed to increase capacity and resulted in better performance and delivery of state services, the prioritization of capacity building over democratization unleashed social crises, which ultimately set the stage for a call for the restoration of stability and hence, paradoxically, a growing quest for bureaucratic rule.

These two paradoxes would have been addressed through broad power distribution in an inclusive and plural political setting. The choice

Table 2
Varieties of Power and Rule in Turkey

	Distribution of Power	
	Narrow	*Broad*
Authoritarianism	Coercive	Chaotic/fragmented
Pluralism	Patronage-based/clientelistic	Democratically consolidated

Source: Based on Daron Acemoğlu and James A. Robinson, *Why Nations Fail: The Origins of Power, Prosperity, and Poverty* (New York: Crown, 2012).

of narrow power distribution in the Turkish case is the result of the state elite's search for hegemony and dominance over society. The distaste for sharing power and authority is a result of the conservative belief in defending state authority as an exclusive prerogative of state agents, with an underlying mistrust of society. In the Turkish case, broad distribution of power generally ends in chaos and fragmentation. However, such a situation occurs mostly under the straining imperatives of deep divisions and polarization in society, which are direct results of authoritarian rule. The ideal scenario for transforming the state into a service provider and instrument of good governance is to have broad power distribution in a plural political environment.[8] The absence of this condition in the Turkish case is one of the main reasons that state crises recur, mainly as a result of an accumulated inability to perpetuate the clientelist and populist distribution of public goods under a monopolistic hold of power (see table 2).

Unfolding the Crisis after July 15

The most recent state crisis in Turkey was built against this backdrop. Yet it also possessed peculiar elements that further complicated proper functioning of the state apparatus. The AKP's coming to power in 2002 symbolized the culmination of post–Cold War attempts to modernize the government-bureaucracy relationship, which went back to the time of former political leaders Süleyman Demirel and Turgut Özal and the subsequent coalitions in the 1990s. With an empowering electoral mandate, the AKP felt obliged to orchestrate long-awaited reform in the state apparatus. To that end the government espoused a gradualist and indirect approach, co-opting the EU process to neutralize the bureaucratic resistance to reform.[9] The idea of Europeanization thus not only empowered the government to liberalize the administrative system, but also brought together a broad coalition of Islamists, liberals, and moderate Kurds.

Between 2002 and 2004, Turkey experienced an intense process of harmonization with the *acquis communautaire* in order to proceed with its EU membership goal. The secular elements in the bureaucracy were won over, and even the military gave a nod to further the Atatürkist ideal of grasping contemporary (Western) civilization. The EU process proved to be a double-edged sword, whereby a practical package of state reform was introduced to bring efficiency to the administrative system together with derogations compromising state sovereignty. Overall, the EU process "established new mechanisms to make public administration more transparent, accountable and participatory."[10]

The ensuing controversy in Turkey was not about allegiance to the EU process but about the disagreement on how far the bureaucratic establishment was willing to comply with the electoral mandate. The presidential elections in 2007, wherein the parliament was poised to elect former deputy prime minister and minister of foreign affairs Abdullah Gül, turned into a major crisis. The military issued an ultimatum because Gül's family was seen as unfit to represent the secular values of the Republic. There were massive demonstrations by secularists all over Turkey against the AKP's choice and a great deal of concern that the Republic was under threat from Islamists taking over the presidency, especially after holding on to the posts of the premier and the speaker of the parliament—the top three positions in terms of state protocol.[11] The AKP espoused a two-way response to overcome the crisis: first, to call snap elections and, second, to co-opt the Gülenists to break bureaucratic resistance. The latter choice, as was proven by the later course of events, laid the groundwork for an even broader political and institutional crisis in the state apparatus.

The Gülenists, who gained predominance in the top echelons of the state through a feeling of esprit de corps, utilized their growing bureaucratic, economic, and media power to delegitimize the secular stronghold on the state system. The AKP appeared willing to yield to the Gülenist project as the party came to the brink of closure and political ban in 2008. After being declared the linchpin of antisecular activities in Turkey, the AKP could only avert the ban with a five-to-four Constitutional Court vote that nevertheless issued monetary punishment for such activities as a warning notice. Once more, legal and political disputes turned into existential conflicts that could have unraveled the political system. The deputy head of the AKP, Mahir Ünal, identifying the problematic relations between his party and the Gülenists, states: "While we tried to strengthen civil space, it turned out that we jumped out of the frying pan into the fire, because an illegal organization, which presented itself as legal, started to in the meantime infiltrate the state."[12] In other words, the political decision to break the ranks of the military bureaucracy through dubious and mostly unsubstantiated court cases, the Ergenekon and Sledgehammer (*Balyoz*) trials, brought about the Gülenists' virtual takeover of the military, judiciary, and police.

The presumptuous division of labor in the aftermath of the 2010 constitutional referendum, whereby the AKP held political power and the Gülenists acquired bureaucratic power, proved unsustainable. The latter had proved reckless in employing state authority to eliminate the strongholds of the secular bureaucracy and had further eroded the Turkish state's institutional capacity. The scorched-earth tactics of the Gülenists, who were declared a terrorist organization (FETÖ, Fethullahist Terror Organization) by the Turkish courts in 2014, unwound the uniformity of state authority. The Gülenist cadres in the bureaucracy, in a complicated relationship with AKP, followed a multipronged attempt to obtain monopoly of the state by cheating on entrance exams and in interviews, interfering with appointments and promotions, and sidelining potential rivals through threat, intimidation, eavesdropping, and similar dirty tactics. The July 15 failed coup attempt looked like the Gülenists' last resort to turn the tables against the ongoing purges in the bureaucracy, which aimed to eliminate their disruptive attempt to neutralize governmental authority.[13]

Since then Turkey has entered yet another phase of redefining the government-bureaucracy relationship. The AKP circles have contended that a strong presidency would eradicate the tutelary power of the bureaucracy and pave the way for efficient and representative government. The proposed system, which was put to referendum on April 16, 2017, resulted in presidential control of the bureaucracy, whereby the cadres in top echelons would be appointed every five years according to the president's choice. It also turned the Council of Ministers into a council of technocrats, responsible and accountable only to the president, without parliamentary oversight. This marked a paradigmatic shift in public administration toward a sui generis Turkish model.

Two fundamental questions arise about the feasibility of this change: first, the basis of bureaucratic upbringing and, second, the bureaucracy's ethos and performance criteria. The modern bureaucracy in Turkey has been a product of Western education, and during the Republican era the state opted for continuity by upholding that choice. In that sense, institutions such as Harbiye and Mülkiye maintained their status as breeding grounds for the military and civilian bureaucracy, respectively. The AKP government, in its fifteen-year rule, has been unable to establish similar institutions, let alone a purposeful education policy.

An even more overarching question would be about the defining ethos and performance criteria in the bureaucracy. In practice, partisanship has brought nothing but nepotism, favoritism, and clientelism in public administration, which had been partly offset by the institutional setup of the Republican era. For example, the university and high school exams had been one of the most egalitarian outlets that enabled lower- and middle-class citizens to seek vertical mobility in Turkey. In fact, the AKP and conservative elites are products of this egalitarian aspect of the Republic, which presented an option to balance against bureaucratic exclusivity in Republican institutions, in terms of either social roots or ideology. If the emerging bureaucratic ethos is to serve the governing party, this would entail ideological and institutional sophistication, which has been an acknowledged failure of the AKP.[14] The most likely scenario ahead is a painful transition process that would entail education and indoctrination of the new cadres from scratch with yet-to-be-established institutions and norms.

In the aftermath of the coup attempt, the political class and the bureaucracy have been alarmed over the destructive effects of the state crisis. Since breaking away from the *Millî Görüş* line, the AKP government has had in the back of its mind the potential threat of the military-civilian bureaucracy intervening in the political process. The main opposition party, the Republican People's Party (CHP), and cornerstones of the Republican regime such as the military, judiciary, and mainstream secular media have been preemptively accused of being complicit in the possibility of such a rupture. In order to avert the sword of Damocles above its rule, the AKP has sought comprehensive reform and promoted its case for transition to a presidential system.[15] Therefore, the actual turn of events was construed as a vindication of the AKP's projections. In the wake of the coup attempt, despite the AKP's semblance of being in control, the underlying motive behind its will to transition was to have maximum political control in order to avert the recurring threat of coups d'état. While still assured about its electoral power, the AKP leadership has been concerned about the possibility of nonelectoral, tutelary forces disrupting the political process. Hence the constitutional cure of a Turkish-type presidential system, first to ensure majoritarian control of all levers of the government, transcending the separation of powers, and second to sideline bureaucratic resistance by remodeling it.

Although the military and civilian bureaucracy have taken a severe hit through the course of events, including purges, the bureaucracy felt vindicated when civilian and uninformed political choices brought the state to the brink of collapse, prompting the quest for restoration of bureaucratic rule to reinstate state power. The conservative elements in the bureaucracy have largely been either purged or sidelined, and the higher echelons of the bureaucracy are again filled by pre-2010 nationalist-secular elements who saw the July 15 purges as a second chance to resuscitate what they considered their entitlement to power.[16] However, the debilitated bureaucracy lacks political and international support, and more important, it has lost the allegiance of traditional allies; namely, the bourgeoisie and local elites and landowners. Therefore, a best-case scenario for the medium term is cohabitation during an inevitable process of transition toward a new political order.[17]

Institutional Reform

The triggering domestic and international factors facilitated a systemic shift toward a consolidated political system with stronger executive powers, which was deemed essential for Turkey, according to President Erdoğan.[18] In this sense, political principles play a crucial role in determining the course and direction of reform. As Andrew Cortell and Susan Peterson argue, political leaders "occupy and control the reins of government and thus possess the means to enforce their preferences."[19] Other actors, like bureaucracy and society, become influential in the reform process in relation to their proximity and level of access to political rulers. According to President Erdoğan, the need for greater state capacity is the reason behind the search for change to the presidential system in Turkey. In a prereferendum rally Erdoğan underlined the de facto transition to a new administrative system, which has to be put in the flesh: "Whether one accepts it or not, Turkey's administrative system has changed. Now, what should be done is to update this de facto situation in the legal framework of the constitution."[20]

Bureaucrats should, to a certain extent, have their own motivations for providing public services independent of the political preferences of the ruling elite. Furthermore, bureaucrats require partial autonomy from the elected government to provide policy advice as well as policy implementation. They also need to have incentives to contribute to cultivating public goods for citizens in order to safeguard the legitimacy of the state.[21] Although these two premises separate the government's will from that of the bureaucracy, and are likely to be the case in Turkey, civil servants in general are cognizant of the need for reform, capacity, and institution-building in the state apparatus,[22] even if to substantiate the abovementioned motives.

In the case of significant state reform, the state's capacity would result either in administrative capacity supplementing democratic consolidation or in coercive power advancing autocracy.[23] According to Michael Mann, coercive power is the "range of actions which the elite is empowered to undertake without routine, institutionalized negotiation with civil society groups."[24] The state's capacity would also appropriate an alternative preference to democratic consolidation to "penetrate civil society and to implement logistically political decisions throughout the realm."[25]

Ultimately the massive purges in the aftermath of the failed July 15 coup have doubled the depressing need for administrative reform, which would have to take into account the abovementioned background of government-bureaucracy relationship. Moreover, there is ample room for reformist leaders to maneuver in order to adapt and implement a reform agenda in Turkey. This is largely because state reform is indeed projected as both the justification for and the result of the search for systemic change as a political project.

Lifetime bureaucrats may serve longer than the politicians, and they would like to preserve their collective and individual interests as parts and makers of the state machine. This does not mean that bureaucrats may not have political positions and negotiate with the rulers for facilitating their services. However, Turkey's ruling party wants to keep the bureaucracy at arm's length and pursue reform goals through systemic change from parliamentary to presidential rule. There is still enough reason and motivation on the side of the bureaucracy to interact with the rulers in order to facilitate services and benefits for their own bureau in Turkey. Thus the widespread agreement on the need for reform legitimizes the institutional rearrangements. The challenge here is that institutional rearrangements can generate greater infrastructural power or secure loyalist political and economic interests. The envisioned systemic change runs the risk of empowering the elected president to use changes in an institutional setting to consolidate the president's hold on power and eliminate and undermine existing political constellations toward a monopolistic political order.

The way in which the state's capacity was challenged has played a decisive role in shaping the mindset of the ruling elite when it is developing policies in the post–July 15 era. Orçun Selçuk argues, "As Turkish state capacity is increasingly challenged by Kurdish separatists and Islamic extremists, the experiences of Venezuela and Ecuador are highly instructive, particularly with regard to their high rates of murder, political violence and the emergence of violent non-state actors."[26] One member of the Turkish parliament underlines a different perspective: "Competitive economic development, political stability, effective governance, and the fight on the multiple fronts against the terrorist groups requires greater state power. Though it may seem coercive, that is what Turkey needs at this time."[27] The direction of the use of state power will depend on how relevant actors handle institutional rearrangement under the imperatives of state crisis after July 15.

The way in which projected systemic change will transform public administration institutions is also not clear at the moment. However, there is an overall perspective on how public administration will take shape in the coming years. The assumed time period for change and transformation has been set as the period between the April 16, 2017, referendum and June 24, 2018, presidential elections.[28] The referendum has thus been conceived as a mandate to implement bureaucratic reform. The top bureaucratic posts will be changed to managerial positions and filled by political appointees for the period of the elected presidency.[29] According to Özlem Zengin, chief advisor to president, this change in principle aims to fulfill the criteria of policy consistency and accountability in the administration.[30] The permanent bureaucracy or state establishment will consist of junior and midlevel civil servants who will not be subject to reshuffling, with a view to maintaining an element of continuity in public administration.

The harmony between political consistency and bureaucratic autonomy underlines an intrinsic dilemma between bureaucracy and government in Turkey. Namely, the bureaucrat "is expected to be both independent and subservient, both responsible for its actions and subject to ministerial responsibility, both politicized and non-politicized at the same time."[31] However, defeating the bureaucratic stronghold through institutional reform will depend on bridging the gap between the ambitions of the government and the capacity and willingness of the bureaucrats to appropriate new roles. There would likely be tension between the political appointees and other civil servants and possible adaptation problems for adjusting the roles toward a functional public administration. The proponents of the presidential system contend that the electoral mandate and political appointments would allow top bureaucrats to better respond to the public demand for reform. Again, it would still render a certain degree of bureaucratic autonomy to the junior and midlevel civil servants under the gaze of the clientelistic political culture in Turkey.

Bureaucratic reform will certainly aim to increase the state's capacity to deal with a variety of problems, ranging from separatist threats to the quality of education. Turkish politicians blame the bureaucratic cadres for failing to address a number of problems. That is why there is a continuous search for capacity development and a better functioning state system.[32] On the side of civil servants, rather than involvement at the micro and macro level of issues and problems, their bureaucratic socialization and bureau culture shapes the ethos and skills of the organization.[33] Both institutional ethos and self-interest play an important role in shaping the bureaucratic functions of the office. In other words, while certain norms define a bureaucratic organization to an extent, salary, promotion, reputation, recognition, and other factors determine what bureaucrats want and how they act in their bureau.[34] Thus the search for a performance- and delivery-oriented public administration will make sense in the state apparatus only if there is a modus vivendi between political and state elites, or if the political elite is able to develop a strong mandate vis-à-vis the latter with congruous internal and external conditions for reform.

State of Reform or State of Emergency

In the context of this pressing call for state reform, Turkey entered into a vicious cycle of political crises in the post–July 15 era. Early hints at cross-party consensus gave way to polarization and widening of the gap between the government and the opposition. Worse still, not only have the confines of opposition been expanded to include differences of opinion within the AKP ranks, but also dissidence has largely become associated with treachery and even terrorism. The government espoused an escalating approach to corner and isolate any attempt to moderate, let alone oppose, its rule under the state of emergency.

This polarizing attitude defied the ordinary dynamics of reform. The April 16 referendum turned into a vote not on the presidential system but on President Erdoğan and his mandate for prospective change. Afterward, with a de facto–uncodified presidential system in place, the thin line between the AKP and the state apparatus became invisible. The president assumed a direct and publicly visible role in policy making, seemingly reflected at all levels of government. This pretense of what Soner Çağaptay calls "Sultanic"[35] rule hinted at an evolving monopolistic political order.

Yet neither the authoritarian policies nor the AKP's hegemonic electoral power ensured an end to tutelary practices in Turkey. Beyond popularized policy decisions, the government appeared far from having authoritative control over the rebooted bureaucratic order, court cases, and transfers of wealth, which tarnished the Turkish state's domestic and international reputation. The perception that dissidents were criminalized, and that intellectuals and journalists were either ostracized or imprisoned for largely unsubstantiated felonies found a receptive audience among both the domestic opposition and international media.[36] Overall, this was construed as an intellectual cleansing to ward off ideological threats in the context of the new Turkish state in the making, which was also the case in earlier postcoup state-building practices.[37] The government unrealistically seemed to think these dynamics were playing into its goal of bringing back political and economic stability. Consequently, beyond the stated aim of freeing the public and private arenas from subversive influences, such as the Gülenists and PKK elements, the criminalizing environment broadly undermined political and social trust in general and also disaffected the pro-AKP groupings, including the conservative and Kurdish electorate in particular.

Under heavy pressure from the political cadres to implement party and government policies without necessarily a prerequisite of legality or precedence, the bureaucracy seemed obliged to take self-preserving measures to protect institutional coherence and sustainability, to ensure the functionality of defensible institutions. The bureaucracy thus wove a web of internal short circuits to preserve its institutional core following massive purges. Yet these moves largely lacked political and democratic mandate. The attempt to restore traditional practices free from legal ordinances was far from legitimate, let alone transparent and accountable. Thus hiring and firing, as well as performance criteria and promotions, became more and more subjective and fed into an ideal of a return to the good old days of bureaucratic hegemony. This general motive has been called a reboot to factory settings, the bureaucratic reflex to restore and uphold the status quo ante. The controversial national public administration examination system was shelved to open up places for trustable staff with ideological and cultural conformity. Powerful yet controversial cliques targeted by the Gülenists in early 2010 made a comeback. Policy dissent or alternative thinking simply became irrelevant. In general, a fait accompli approach again turned into a pervasive characteristic of the bureaucratic cadres, even if restricted in general to the inner workings of the bureaucratic apparatus due to heavy governmental pressures in public policy making.

Particularistic interests also gained an upper hand. The progovernment political cliques acquired a cover of infallibility, leading purges, appointments, and further security checks at all levels of governmental and even societal institutions. The progovernment media, with a strong army of social media outlets, set the tone for the postcoup investigations and court cases. Even intraparty power rivalries turned into media and information wars. The use of prolonged pretrial detention, local courts' resistance to following the decisions of higher courts, noncompliance with European Court of Human Rights verdicts, and political blasts on the courts are main problems of Turkey's judicial system. Furthermore, the enigmatic ultranationalists started bragging about their consolidated hold on bureaucratic cadres and their imprint on the court cases.[38] The Nationalist Action Party (MHP) played an overarching role in defining Turkish foreign and counterterrorism policies, with a growing irredentist tone. The Islamic mystic orders (*tarikat*) reportedly gained control of certain sectors of the government and the bureaucracy.[39]

In the end it would not be too far to depict the current imbroglio in the government-bureaucracy relationship as a security dilemma. The government is still apprehensive about possible extralegal executive interventions in its electoral right to rule.[40] The bureaucracy generally has concerns about the viability of the current model of government, which is open to perpetual crises and devoid of any clear prospects about the role and mandate of the bureaucracy. Thus the ideal of state reform as a result of government and bureaucracy cohabitation is largely gone. Therefore, we might rather witness power plays between an ideal of all-encompassing bureaucratic shake-up and a return to bureaucratic rule in Turkey, which appears to be the only alternative in the context of growing political fragmentation in Turkish politics. This presumption does not disregard the fact that higher echelons of the bureaucracy have sworn allegiance, or rather are paying lip service, to the emerging presidential system in place. However, the eradication of the secular bureaucracy that the systemic transformation to the presidential system implies is likely to usher in a period of final reckoning, whereby the government would seek a free hand in political transition, given that it has a five-year mandate to transform the remaining pillars of the ancient regime.

In any case, the ultimate casualty of this disorder and test of wills has been the ideal of state reform. Right after the coup attempt, the idea of consensual government was pronounced by all political parties but was eclipsed too quickly. The unprecedented rally 'round the flag effect was instantly consumed and gave way to partisan rivalry in the presidential referendum held on April 16. Even the postreferendum era has not engendered a reform agenda. Instead, the political parties have sailed full steam toward a new cycle of elections. Reform in this sense came to mean preparing the groundwork for winning the elections in 2018 and, most recently, the municipal elections in 2019—a pragmatic reconceptualization to politicize the idea of reform as well as to defy the need for it. The government continued to prolong the mood of the state of emergency after lifting it and depended more and more on rule by presidential decrees. The opposition upheld a vow to restore the parliamentary regime.[41]

The dualistic structure of an all-powerful presidency without constitutional checks or mechanisms of accountability certainly undid the earlier parliamentary constitutional order. Yet the definition of government organs; the prerogatives of the president, parliament, and judiciary; bureaucratic reform; civil rights; and other constitutional issues pertaining to government have been left in limbo and are yet to replace the imprint of earlier parliamentary practices. The cross-party constitutional reform committee was suspended, and the public debate on the elements of political transition for one reason or another slipped away. The judicial system virtually ceased to function properly following the purges and ongoing investigations, and has proved a nonplayer for stemming the rising propensity for arbitrary and unaccountable executive practices.

Turkey has lost track of the reform process and focused rather on electoral cycles as a means of achieving the political mandate for a renewed constitutional order. Turkish politics have become ever more fragmented between supporters of a yet-to-be defined presidential order and advocates of a return to the parliamentary system. The end result has been the loss of any remnants of consensual politics and common ground. On top of that, the administrative order has lost its proper functioning against the backdrop of purges, infighting, and lack of judicial and effective executive scrutiny. Rather than building a new constitutional and institutional order, the political squabbles in Turkey undid the old order without putting in place the pillars of a new one.

Conclusion

Turkey is facing a major challenge to set the contours of the new presidential system. The lack of ownership of the new system, except for the governing AKP and its coalition partner, the MHP, has left many issues unaddressed and the system's prospects for long-term sustainability in question. The government opted for a dubious route of employing the transition as both an electoral program and a political goal to seal its hegemonic role in the political order. Therefore, the presidential system and the ongoing efforts for institutionalization diverted from its original goals, such as efficiency, managerialism, and public administration performance, to an electoral exercise to win the next elections and isolate the political opposition. While the government cadres turned defensive and tried to make the best out of the emerging order to win the electoral cycles, this short-termism also brought into question the bureaucracy's long-term investment in the emerging system.

The initial hints about the workings of the presidential system effectively call for rethinking this short-termism. Without a clearly defined division of labor between the government and the bureaucracy, there emerges nothing but confusion, stagnation, and ultimate grey zones ruled by arbitrariness and specific interests. As government circles have conceded, the need for rethinking is urgent.[42] Not only the bureaucracy, but also political cadres have lost direction and purpose. Trying to tame the bureaucracy for its political goals, the government seems to have suffocated its operation and its raison d'être. The current ethos in the bureaucracy is defined, above all, by a determination not to make any mistakes and to avert personal risks in the still undefined transition. The presidential committees and newly constituted councils are far from substituting for the policy-making role of the former constitutional order. Even worse, the new political regime has yet to produce a new constitution that would define the roles and prerogatives of the constitutional organs with a broad vision. It has simply been a cut-and-paste exercise to change the body of the 1982 constitution and assign extended and, in general, unsupervised roles to the president at the expense of the parliament.

Growing awareness about the need for an update and overhaul of the new system is an asset. It needs to be used to bring three missing elements back into the new constitutional order. First, the division of labor between the government and bureaucracy needs to be clearly and legally defined. Second, the bureaucratic ethos to maintain a long-term vision beyond electoral cycles needs to be restored. And third, the government should introduce performance criteria and benchmarks to get the bureaucracy to work in accord with its political mandate and its accountability vis-à-vis the electorate. In the end, a government-bureaucracy accord with a certain degree of separation of authority, and autonomy for the latter, is inevitable if the presidential system is to assume a measure of efficiency, responsiveness, accountability, and transparency—the main indicators of good governance.

3

The Role of State in Conflict Resolution in Turkey

In general, states are considered consequential actors in conflict resolution. Beyond the binary analysis of success versus failure, the motivations, persisting attitudes, flexibility and adaptability, learning process, and other factors should be taken into account for grasping the dynamics of the wider conflict resolution role of the state and its conflict transformation capability. In the Turkish case, the fact that the Turkish state is a strong state relative to all domestic actors would imply a relatively smooth field in terms of conflict settlement. Yet in practice this assumption is not verified when it comes to addressing major political, social, ideational and ethnic conflicts. This is largely due to the state elite's failure to grasp the dynamics and complexity of conflict resolution, which has resulted in the simplistic practice of employing either co-optation or coercion, rather than accommodation, as exclusive formulas in the domestic arena.

Against this backdrop, this chapter observes the role of state in conflict resolution in Turkey in a wider political context. It analyzes the status and problems of the state conflict resolution roles and the ways to address these problems as part of the larger state crisis in Turkey. The evolution of the state conflict resolution roles under a new government system, if any, would provide significant insight into the future course of state action vis-à-vis the conflict situations in Turkey. This chapter addresses the following questions. What is the role of the Turkish state in conflict resolution? What defines this role? In what ways do conflict resolution roles differ in domestic and foreign policy? What are the repercussions of these roles? Did the conflict resolution roles change after systemic transition to presidential rule? This chapter underlines the need for change in the state's conflict resolution role for provision of vital public goods of security and stability, and offers constructive steps for a political and cultural shift in conflict resolution.

Politics, Power, and State in Turkey

The Turkish state tradition was largely shaped by early modernization attempts that aimed at building a capable state authority. In a continuum, the process of state building not only defined the political direction of the country but also shaped the very dynamics of the state system, which eventually gave rise to the modern nation-state. Overall the patrimonial belief that "the well-being of the society depended upon the well-being of the state"[1] was largely held as a founding premise in Turkish political thought. This state-centric outlook that sought to empower the state vis-à-vis domestic and external actors has given the state elites major, if not exclusive, roles as agents of change in Turkey.

Historically the leader of the state has had exclusive rights over the realm, to the degree of assuming divine authority,[2] which reflexively also elevated the future role of executive leaders beyond the limits of constitutional and electoral politics. Following modernization, the bureaucracy aptly gained an upper hand in duplicating the Westernizing reforms and turned into agents of further centralization of state authority.[3] The rise of what has been called "the modern administrative state"[4] paved the way for centralization and, more precisely, competitive hold of state authority between the political leadership and civil bureaucracy, the latter more and more assuming a self-assigned role as the guardian of the state.

Owing to the innate populist characteristics of the Republican regime and the ensuing democratizing reforms, popular legitimacy has been a defining element of the system. Therefore, the inherent "center-periphery"[5] dichotomy in Turkish politics, between the ruling strata and the populace, necessitated the integration of public grievances in the political system. Yet again, policy making remained a privileged mandate for the state elites, who sustained their hold on state authority in the name of the state's supreme and even transcendental interests. In any case, civil society or pluralistic pressure groups either were too vulnerable to the state's command or opted to embed themselves in the state apparatus. They mostly attempted to raise their voices when they felt secure enough to shape public opinion and influence policy.

The Turkish state has largely been successful in integrating majority groups into its fold, never turning itself into a postcolonial-type minority regime. The early Republican years saw a relatively smooth transition from the millet system to renaming the Muslim majority, with the inclusion of major immigrant groups from the Balkans, Middle East, and Caucasus as (Muslim) Turks. The founders of the Republic were largely former Young Turks. Thus their immigrant roots were juxtaposed to their elite status, thanks to their educational backgrounds in the Ottoman academies. They embarked on a civilizing mission to modernize the Anatolian people with transformative steps toward Westernization and Turkification. Later on the Republic, in different phases, came to integrate the Anatolian peasantry and Muslim petite bourgeoisie through either urbanization or education. In the end, regardless of their ethnic or rural background, the cultural center defined by the state elites picked up capable and willing peripheral elements, who later on became the stalwarts of the Republican regime in either politics, the military, or the bureaucracy. Yet this openness to personal vertical mobility did not amount to integration of peripheral culture into the center.

Overall, the tone of political competition was set by the rivalry for power among the state elites. Against a backdrop of shifting alliances between domestic and external actors, elected governments faced the formidable authority of the civil and military bureaucracy. The relative weight of these two major actors defined the autocratic or pluralistic character of the political regime. With a claim to ideological ownership of the regime, and given long-term professional security, the bureaucracy, in default mode, opted to settle for a seemingly behind-the-scenes role in a balance-of-power setting. Unless a strong party, government, or leader with ample political legitimacy pushed the political system to its limits, the bureaucratic apparatus shied away from forfeiting such a guardian role. Only in the disequilibrium of a quest for political hegemony, which would again occur in the form of either strong political leadership or uncontested bureaucratic transitions at times of rupture, would the possibility of autocratic administration increase. In the modern Turkish experience, the latter case did not last long, and the bureaucracy would seek to set the constitutional limits of the system following major political adjustments, such as the military coups almost every decade, in which the military put binding checks in place and withdrew to its supervisory role afterward.

The tension between the state elite's centralizing reforms and the periphery's quest for autonomy also determined the cooperative or coercive tone of the relationship between the state and society. The Republican ideals of modernizing the nation in a top-down fashion, which at the end of the day isolated Islam in the public sphere as a "backward" belief of the periphery, aggravated the dichotomy between what Mardin calls "the bureaucratic center" and "the democratic periphery."[6] Thereafter, Turkish political parties entered into an unending power struggle against these structural dynamics. With the bureaucracy's unwavering hold on Republican values, above all *laïcité* and nationalism, the periphery's pluralistic and popular striving to legitimize its worldview through electoral politics largely hit a wall. A series of military coups under the straitjacket of the Cold War sustained this bureaucratic hegemony in defining the state ideology, hence the rules of the game.

Only in a post–Cold War setting could the periphery take incremental steps to turn around this equation. Beginning with the liberalist reforms of former president Turgut Özal (1983–89 as prime minister and 1989–93 as president), conservative-nationalist parties vying for peripheral support paved the way for integrating the symbols of Islam—more precisely, Islamism—into mainstream Turkish politics. On that note, the Justice and Development Party (AKP) along the lines of the Democratic Party (DP) of the 1950s and Justice Party (AP) of the 1960s, made yet another attempt to democratize the bureaucratic center. The party found international backing thanks to a series of favorable developments, above all the European Union (EU) accession process, as well as the post–9/11 international conjuncture. However, in the context of an entrenched political regime, consequential electoral support for the AKP did not amount to a predominant role. Rather the political rivalry carried on with military ultimatums, party closure threats, and alleged coup plans.

Yet, the AKP's response to this undemocratic resistance has not been exclusively democratic, as its proponents claim. On the contrary, it committed a cardinal sin when it co-opted the unruly elements in the security and judicial apparatus to rollback what they dubbed bureaucratic tutelage. This diversion to extralegal and, in general, illegitimate methods undid the AKP's founding ethos to represent a universal appeal for democratizing the regime. Shaky and unsustainable coalitions working toward mostly short-term goals derailed the party's unique chance to liberalize the system. In the end, rather than bringing together peripheral elements and solidifying a consensual democratic center, the AKP came to redefine and own the bureaucratic center on its own terms, more recklessly following the July 15 coup attempt in 2016. With the rise of multivectoral security threats, the AKP government came to co-opt the security state and chose to coerce oppositional elements, mainly the dissident secularists and the centrifugal Kurds, into submission.

The major question for Turkey's future conflict map was whether the newly defined center would inadvertently solidify a democratic or rejectionist periphery. The answer to this question would also be telling about the direction of democratic politics in Turkey. In case of a sustained legitimacy problem, the loss of a delicate balance in the center-periphery dichotomy could turn Turkey into what Kalevi Holsti calls a "weak state" and push the door wide open for internal conflict. One could reemphasize Holsti's advice to "strengthen the states" to reestablish both the eroding state capacity and political legitimacy in Turkey.[7] Therefore, Turkish policy makers are better advised to rethink and reframe conflict resolution as an instrument of political legitimacy in Turkish politics.

Conflict Resolution Roles of The Turkish State

Against this background of political competition in Turkey, the state has assumed definitive conflict resolution roles in domestic and foreign policy. The variance in tone and methodology stems naturally from the differences in jurisdiction and sovereignty rights at home and in the foreign realm. Examining the choices of policy makers and their varying roles provides additional information about the principles and mechanisms of the Turkish state's conflict resolution efforts. Although the state's conflict resolution role is dynamic in nature, state choices rely on deep-seated preferences, and necessities are contingent on developments on domestic, regional, and international fronts. Turkey's state tradition and national security agenda prevail in the determination of the state's conflict resolution roles.

The state's traditionally predominant role in the domestic sphere is thought to assign it an all-out role in conflict resolution. However, the major determinant of conflict resolution efforts is not the conventional role assumed by the state, but the autocratic or pluralistic character of the regime, which is largely a function of the government-bureaucracy relationship. The more the accord between the two, the better the chances of the state's capacity to transform the conflict situation, which would seal the efficiency of conflict resolution efforts. The idea behind transforming the situation is to achieve a lasting and participatory solution to the conflict. In case of autocratic administration—strong political leadership or an uncontested bureaucratic regime—the state is less likely to be open for dialogue, compromise, or integration of public grievances. Therefore, absent the magic formula of a pluralistic relationship between the government-bureaucracy and society, the Turkish state's conflict resolution role is predominantly defined under the binary choices of co-optation and coercion, leaving accommodation aside as an option. Moreover, even at times of pluralistic harmony, the so-called state memory (in other words, bureaucratic reflexes) sets certain barriers before political attempts to transform and desecuritize the conflict situation.

Overall, the Turkish state's defining approach to internal conflicts is to defy and delegitimize peripheral activity. There is a thin line between co-optation and coercion as defining alternatives since both use either violence or the threat of violence as leverage. Given that political competition is deemed a zero-sum game, the deep-rooted state tradition is intolerant of opposition of any kind. This equation accepts no exception in times of crisis, and even decent attempts to contribute to conflict resolution roles by third parties carry the risk of being construed as undermining the state's authority. As one media representative underlined: "Although civil society attempts to open a maneuvering space in the political arena, it would only be possible by the will and consent of the state, which is the determinant actor" in Turkey.[8] In this sense, civil society and citizens are taught to help themselves out of conflict situations within the straitjacket of existing state institutions, and boundaries set by the state apparatus.

The state's nonconciliatory conflict resolution roles of co-optation and coercion are mainly due to a perpetuated refusal to establish and manage a working relationship with society under an inclusive social order. In theory, co-optation creates opportunity for accommodation of differences and ideally embeds peripheral demands in relevant institutions. Repression is the state's capacity for coercion. Although the Turkish state has exhibited an integrative capacity in a number of cases, such as the Kurdish peace process and the Alevi (Alawite) opening, these attempts did not go beyond tactical steps and played into political exigency rather than symbolizing strategic orientation toward reconciliation. The state-government dichotomy diminished the government's political control over structural conflicts, including the Kurdish problem, and usually ended up referring those issues to the security establishment as their exclusive zone of authority and expertise.[9] Early hopes at the outset of these recent conflict resolution efforts have turned into further disappointment without substantial improvement to change the conflict situation and to thaw their structural traits. Regardless of the initial choice of co-optation or coercion, the state reserves the penal right to criminalize its domestic interlocutors and to write them off as nonplayers in conflict resolution processes at any point. On the other hand, the state's incoherent and haphazard application of coercion, together with insufficient capacity for addressing peripheral demands, has resulted in protracted and, in most cases, frozen conflicts in Turkey. Turkish administrations in general and the AKP governments in particular have demonstrated that they may not prioritize conflict resolution unless the conflicts escalate into a potential national security threat or resolution will serve their immediate political agenda.

There has been a cycle of securitization and desecuritization in terms of the state's approach to so-called internal enemies. The enemy-threat chain and repudiation of peripheral demands is the preference of the state, almost in a default mode. The state's failure to build up political and societal consent for policies through participation and good governance results in reproduction of partition (*bölünme*) paranoia and imposition of a perpetual mood of a state of emergency in daily lives.[10] The exceptional periods of relative desecuritization result in deescalation of the conflicts and provide the state relief in its domestic and international conflict resolution roles. Such eras of lowered threat perception have mostly overlapped with periods of Turkish realignment in foreign policy to accommodate the pressing need for harmony with the ascendant international order. Absent foreign pressures for change or during international periods of upheaval, the dominant mode of a national security state duly sets in. At such times nuanced understanding of conflicts in a pluralistic center-periphery relationship is generally missing. This also empowers a monolithic understanding of politics and leads to labeling the opposition as a threat to national security. It is a matter of time before the forces of opposition face reprisals without an objective understanding of either their crime or of why some entities are exposed to state measures while others are spared or sidelined without punishment.

For the Turkish state, it does not matter whether the conflict is societal, ethnic, confessional, or of any other nature. There are no signs of a learning process taking root, considering the fact that the national security state apparatus has sustained a nonconciliatory approach without much success in defusing crises. An orthodox loyalty to the state's traditional conflict resolution roles can be seen in the state's attitude toward the Kurdish problem, namely the resuscitation of 1990s policies following a series of short-lived peace processes. A similar detour from peace to national security measures was witnessed under President Özal after he granted light recognition to the Kurds and the prospect of peace. Following his death, the talks on ceasefire and solutions left their place to harsh security measures.[11] The assumption in the literature on conflict resolution is that for states "in a prolonged conflict, learning takes place" in accordance with "changes in beliefs, in behavior, and in policy, due to the extent of time and the variety of events included in this type of conflict."[12] Sırrı Süreyya Önder, former member of parliament from the pro-Kurdish People's Democratic Party (HDP) and a high-profile figure during the so-called solution process, responded to a question about what the state apparatus can do for a solution to the Kurdish problem: "What we want from the state is to stay away a little bit from feeding into conflict."[13]

The recurrence of resistance to change and revival of the security state is both structural and cultural. First, it is due mainly to the state's lack of capacity to control various conflict situations. Structurally, the state apparatus is unprepared for conflict resolution roles and continues to defy negotiation processes as a threat to its overall authority. The common toolbox of co-optation and coercion is far from able to secure the conflict parties' cooperation, especially without strict adherence to rule of law and legitimate institutions of trust and accountability.[14] Fikri Sağlar, former member of parliament from Republican People's Party (CHP), pointed out the overlapping attitudes of the ruling AKP with the authoritarian understanding following the 1980 coup. He underscored the exclusion of the Kurds and other peripheral groups in a context of state failure and the rise of authoritarian tendencies in politics.[15]

Second, the state does not have a culture of inclusiveness and openness and does not provide any room for integrating peripheral grievances into the political system. This attitude blocks negotiation channels, even if there would emerge an opportunity to co-opt certain groups. Talip Küçükcan, former member of parliament from the ruling AKP, challenges this view, stating with regard to the public sphere: "Today, there is more opportunity for expressing one's identity in comparison to the past."[16]

However, even if this is so, the state's domestic conflict resolution roles are far from addressing the dynamic nature of the societal, ideational, and ethnic conflicts in Turkey. Societal and nonstate actors "strategically navigate the institutional, spatial, and knowledge politics that produce and transform"[17] conflict situations, which go beyond the predetermined worldview behind the state's conflict resolution roles. As a result, the state's strategies fail to produce counternarratives against societal actors who define the conflict situation and perpetuate their claim outside the purview of the political system. The history of Islamist, leftist, and Kurdish movements epitomize this cycle of repudiation followed by cycles of co-optation or, more often than not, coercion; while only the former Islamists found a way of redefining the bureaucratic center as a result of their later co-optation in the 2000s, again only after espousing a conservative-nationalist discourse arguably in harmony with the state identity.

Thus state-employed conflict resolution measures have been far from able to provide transformative justice in Turkey, while certain segments of society perpetuate, either actively or passively, polarized and deepening memories of conflict. What comes forward instead is the state's commitment to survival at all costs. This existential approach again sets the stage for the vicious circle of self-fulfilling threats and countermoves toward a wide range of enemies in the country—not the processes of forgetting the ramifications of the conflict and making it a matter of the past in societal memory. The state puts forward a power hierarchy through formal means of oppression and expects the obedience and submission of peripheral groups. This also stems from an approach that automatically writes off peripheral demands as inferior and confers to the state apparatus a blank check to bend these demands in its favor. The state's superiority complex leads to a dilemma in which the repeated escalation of threats again feeds into a perceived matter of life or death. Although such enemy-threat chains with exaggerated presentation serve to vindicate the national security agenda of the state apparatus, what matters is the state's capacity, as opposed to incapacity, to deal with the conflict situations in the end.

Problems of the State Conflict Resolution Roles

The validity of conflict management depends on implementing immediate or time-sensitive measures toward a mitigation or transformation of the conflict. The state's conflict resolution roles emanate from, beyond country-specific state traditions, the state's capabilities, choice of uses of power, and strategic environment. In the Turkish case, these conflict resolution roles face three major deficits that inhibit delivery of the desired results vis-à-vis conflicts.

Learning Process

First is the Turkish state's aversion to the learning process. This has particularly been the case with regard to societal conflicts and the state's repeated reactive responses. A much-publicized example is the urban riots in the summer of 2013, which had a major role in tarnishing Turkey's rising international reputation and soft power. The protest of a small environmental group defending the preservation of the Gezi Park, a small green area in central İstanbul, amid rumors that a shopping mall would be built on it, escalated to widespread riots in major cities in Turkey.[18] Instead of working toward a negotiated settlement and getting into dialogue with the groups involved, the state duly introduced coercive measures against the civilian protesters.

The government displayed a high measure of insecurity with its fierce response, even at a time of greatest political security and legitimacy. The message was crystal clear: state authority was not to be compromised, and political demands could not be forced on the state elites. Again, the government's response was reactive and nonconciliatory. This response, in turn, enabled a number of illegal groups to hijack the civilian protests and transgress the limits of civilian disobedience in some cases. Overall, the spillover of the riots across the country, the escalation of violence, and deepening polarization were a nonissue in the eyes of policy makers in terms of measures employed for managing the conflict.

The rising violence on the side of the protesters was used to construct a narrative that enemies of the state were joining their forces to overthrow the Turkish government, and this narrative has been used to justify measures against the protesters. Criminalization, othering, and oppression have constituted the chain of state behavior in response to urban demonstrations, which are not the biggest challenge at state's conflict resolution agenda. The specter of the Gezi events continues to haunt the government, the narrative about which has, ever since, been reframed to back the government's political needs. As a result, the events have come to be associated occasionally with the Gülenists, the United States, the EU, the Kurdistan Workers' Party (PKK), separatists, liberals, independent-minded academics, and the opposition, particularly the CHP leadership. Thus it can also be said that the state's elites have not come to terms with the learning deficit about conflict resolution, even after the events were suppressed and the political mobilization came to an end.

Such an approach was also in play during the protests after a deadly explosion in a coal mine in the town of Soma in May 2014. The worst mining disaster in Turkish history resulted in anger and grief for people in Soma and nationwide. The protests at some point led to security forces' attacks against the protestors, even involving prime minister himself and his cabinet members. This was the same response as in other cases where the thin line between co-optation and coercion by the Turkish state was used as a means of CR.[19]

The State's Peace Plan

The second problem for Turkey's conflict resolution role has been the absence of a peace plan under the umbrella of the state apparatus. The violence-prone and often militarized conflict resolution methods of the Turkish state dominate the field of conflict resolution, no matter whether the conflict is an urban riot or ethnic insurgency. The state's lack of comprehensive and multifaceted conflict resolution roles, and its prioritization of counterterrorism measures, bear responsibility for missed opportunities to pursue a reconciliatory track. Counterterrorism is a matter for the state and requires an administrative level of decision making, while CR is a matter of wider consensus that includes the state and societal actors in a wider political agenda.

There was a brief period of negotiation between the state and an umbrella of Kurdish actors, which also reportedly included certain elements of the PKK terrorist organization in the recent past. It found political and social support across the board, and represented a comprehensive initiative to see the Kurdish problem as a matter of the past. Yet the process was dubious from the beginning. For one, the state elites refrained from calling negotiations with the Kurdish groups a peace process, preferring to call them a solution process as the state's version of defining the situation. The political leadership seemed to have overcome the statist biases but fell into the trap of electoral short-termism, which again conferred to it a tone of co-optation. The government and its negotiation team apparently lacked the state authority's expertise on the Kurdish problem and believed that a discursive shift could transform the conflict situation.

More important, the security apparatus was not engaged in the process and was far from convinced about its long-term viability. With the spill-over of the Syrian conflict and ISIS attacks against the Syrian Kurds, the government's ability to confine the process within a Turkey-only dynamic became untenable. In the end, despite symbolic steps and conciliatory rhetoric, the process failed to fulfill its promise to transform the structural pillars of the conflict.

The choice of shying away from associating with a peace initiative was above all related to the absence of a peace plan; there was a failure to set the terms for the start, development, and conclusion of the process beyond creating a climate of optimism. This approach failed to define the goals and did not offer the public and state elites an acceptable and sustainable formula toward peace. There was also an element of wishful thinking and unpreparedness to transform the conflict situation, another sign of the lack of a learning process. As one bureaucrat indicated, "Security circles in Ankara were not at ease with the AKP's approach to solving the Kurdish problem since the terrorist organization [the PKK] has a free hand, while the solution process hindered security measures and made the state weak against it."[20] The Wise People Commission, the members of which were selected with the approval of both the state authorities and to some extent the Kurdish groups to lead peace talks, entered into dialogue with almost all sections of society to popularize and legitimize peace in public opinion. However, the Wise People's mission ended abruptly despite considerable public outreach. While the hardliners prevailed among the Kurdish groups in favor of expansion in Syria and terror attacks in Turkey, there was discernible resistance from the state establishment and nationalist groups to tolerating the possibility of an auxiliary role for both the eminent persons and the Kurdish negotiators.

According to Sağlar, the ruling AKP exploited the governing position to manipulate the political agenda of transition in order to elevate its party leader to a strong presidential position. He argues that the state elites lacked a conclusive peace plan, specifically about the Kurdish issue, and that the limited number of peace attempts only served particularistic political agendas in Turkey.[21] Mesut Yeğen, a scholar at Istanbul Sehir University, opposes this view and details the role of mismanagement by the parties, which led to an eventual failure in concluding the peace process.[22] According to Ersel Aydınlı and Nihat Ali Özcan, the difficulty of the Kurdish question in Turkey in terms of CR is the existence of an armed faction, which blurs the boundaries between conflict resolution and counterterrorism.[23] The strong belief in the need to have the upper hand with an aura of superiority vis-à-vis peripheral demands prevented both the government and the bureaucracy from taking nuanced steps in conflict management, which ensured failure given that a peace plan for reconciliation was missing in the first place.

Turkish state elites prefer counterterrorism over conflict resolution since the latter pertains to political processes and negotiation, which would imply partial disassociation from the security realm and an overarching role for civilian actors. The preference of employing counterterrorism measures in the widest possible sense in response to conflict situations did not change under the new security structure of the state. The Turkish government chose this approach to dealing with those whom it considered enemies of the state through a nationwide state of emergency in the post–July 15 era. The subsequent emergency decrees and later presidential decrees paved the way for unbridled state power to block any opposition in Turkey.

Institutional Structure

The deficiency of the state's peace plan is also reflective of a third problem: the lack of institutions in the conflict management process. The Undersecretariat of Public Order and Security (Kamu Düzeni ve Güvenliği Müsteşarlığı), operating under the Ministry of Interior, was established in 2010 to strengthen official capacity for conflict management in Turkey. It had, inter alia, the duty of "informing public opinion through national and international works and gaining public support" for counterterrorism activities.[24] The undersecretariat organized the Wise People Commission work all around Turkey in the later months of 2013 and the first half of 2014. After the impasse and eventual eruption of violence in Kurdish-majority areas, this institution was sidelined and no longer played any conflict management role until it was abolished by an executive decree in

July 2018. A second example is that of the General Directorate for Conflict Management and Mediation, which was created by Law 6004 on the Organization and Duties of the Ministry of Foreign Affairs. Despite the critical role of conflict resolution in Turkish foreign policy and a number of mediation initiatives abroad, this general directorate of the ministry has not been operational, and the related issues were still being handled by the policy-planning unit until appointment of a director general as late as January 2019.

The Turkish parliament has not played a prominent role in CR in Turkey either. Aside from political representation issues, due mainly to political party law and the 10 percent electoral threshold for parliamentary representation of political parties, the parliament failed to play a critical role in conflict resolution in Turkey. This had largely to do with the control of the parliament by the majority-holding government parties. Beyond that, a major weakness of the parliament has been an extension of the long-standing characteristic of Turkish political culture that in general rules out accommodation and consensus even on issues of utmost importance. There is a tendency among the politicians from different points on the political spectrum to identify their positions in line with the state apparatus's approach. Therefore, the state elites have had no problem in finding allies in the parliament in their endeavor to pursue a national security–first approach in politics.

The parliament established a steering kind of committee on the peace process in 2013, namely the Solution Process Assessment Commission, with a duty to analyze the ongoing process and to figure out alternatives for increased political participation of different groups, toward the goal of a solution of the Kurdish problem. The commission consisted of eleven members from the AKP and the HDP. Two other parties in the parliament, the CHP and the Nationalist Action Party (MHP), refused to participate in the commission on the grounds that it espoused a separatist agenda and thus stood against national interests. The short-term work of the committee ended up with a comprehensive and progressive report offering analysis of the Kurdish problem and suggesting new perspectives for resolution.[25] The suggestions provided insights for change and for the adoption of new bills to prepare the legal framework for addressing the Kurdish problem in 2014. Despite these radical moves relative to the mainstream conflict resolution attitudes in Turkey, the parliamentary process did not provide substantial input into the peace process and exemplified a broader inability to break the adversarial approaches between the opposition and the government. Strict adherence by the opposition, mainly the CHP and the MHP, to the state's reflexes about the Kurdish question in the context the government's haphazard plans to make a breakthrough was telling about the entrenched position of statist conflict resolution roles in Turkey.

Reorganization of State Institutions and Conflict Resolution Roles

In the process of restructuring the state apparatus in the presidential system, the first presidential decree created an Office of Administrative Affairs directly attached to president that has among its duties to coordinate the activities of domestic security, external security, and counterterrorism in Turkey. There is a General Directorate of Security Affairs under this office, with the task of coordinating policies and strategies of state security with relevant state institutions and following up the implementation of these policies. The Council of Foreign and Security Policies has a responsibility to prepare policy proposals on security issues ranging from natural disasters to cyber security. The presidential system also further weakened the role of the Turkish parliament in the political landscape and its potential to create institutional mechanisms.

The role assignment to security affairs in the presidential government structure does not refer to conflict resolution or a peace perspective and continues the traditional state tendency to treat conflict resolution under the framework of counterterrorism. Furthermore, although the offices were filled by political appointees and selected bureaucrats, they have not become operational yet and would need a certain amount of time to figure out their mandate and responsibilities. Finally, the centralized structure again assigns the president a status overlooking the relevant institutions with overriding power and does not specify his options for delegation of this role. This ambiguous situation challenges the prospect for institutionalization, while seemingly giving the president an opportunity to pursue political projects of conflict resolution beyond the limits of the mainstream approach. The realization of this presidential prerogative will be time-tested, as Turkey has not been able to transcend the climate of a state of emergency since 2016 to operationalize conflict resolution roles in real terms.

In this sense, the restructured state mechanism under the executive presidency does not promise a change in the traditional conflict resolution roles of the state and may instead result in confusion and contradiction in implementation of the vague roles of new offices. The lack of institutionalization persists in the presidential system and appears to be a direct result of the state's preference to treat conflict resolution as an overwhelming security issue and its strong belief in the state's supremacy within the domestic realm. The choices of co-optation and coercion do not require a nuanced approach or institutional expertise. In the long run, the state elites would consider presidential involvement as a challenge and a barrier to managing the conflict situation. The overriding power of an executive president might challenge statist preferences, but it does not necessarily mean emergence of alternative thinking due to the thin line between political choices and state policies in the conflict resolution agenda in Turkey.

Beyond domestic politics, in foreign policy, with a growing need for alternative and specialized processes in conflict resolution, the absence of institutions in policy making is also a reflection of the lack of capacity and expertise on the issues of CR and mediation. Turkey's conflictual geostrategic map entails comprehensive peacemaking and coalition-building processes, as well as sophisticated cadres of negotiators and public diplomacy experts. With erosion in the traditional pillars of foreign-policy making and the presidency's predominant role, a new setting thus appears urgent. Yet the absence of political will, the lack of capacity beyond the traditional actors in foreign-policy making, short-termist political agendas, a contentious political culture, and the state elite's dominant attitudes, inter alia, prevent a paradigm shift in that direction.

Last but not least among major problems facing conflict resolution efforts under the presidential system is the eroding political order in Turkey and difficulty in identifying a unifying ethos for political and social stability. Polarization has become the rule of thumb in Turkish politics. Politicians instrumentalized the failing social contract in order to polarize different segments of society and consolidate their electoral constituencies. Although social groups largely managed to avoid conflict over differences among one another, political and state elites do not hesitate to magnify and deepen polarization as a means of attaining hegemony and control over the state system and, reflexively, society as a whole. Deteriorating government-opposition relations reproduced this unconstructive dynamic in conflict resolution efforts in Turkish domestic and foreign policy.

This motive was also largely the case behind the Gülenist attempts to take over state institutions, which ended in the July 15 coup attempt that eventually brought the state to the point of collapse. The Gülenist understanding of politics has been a product of this polarization, which defies all definitions of rule of law and pluralist democracy. In the end, the terrorizing zero-sum logic not only undermined state institutions but also cultivated further mistrust among different segments of society. Haldun Solmaztürk, director of 21st Century Turkey Institute and retired brigadier general, points to the restraining effect of political polarization and the resultant all-or-nothing tendencies in Turkish politics. He argues that there is no feasible room for constructive attempts at conflict resolution in the current political atmosphere.[26] The poisonous political atmosphere has unwound all elements of the political system in Turkey, and urgently necessitates a broad-based reconciliation for the new structure of the Turkish state to weather the growing instability.

Conclusion

The Turkish state's binary conflict resolution approach of maintaining negative peace has fallen short of resolving complex political and social conflicts in Turkey. This chapter depicts the state's approach and outlines general and specific conflicts to demonstrate the ingrained preference for either co-optation or coercion. This traditional approach, which considers state and society exclusive interlocutors and builds on the belief that state interests trump all others, has failed to comprehend that modern and even post-modern conflicts play out and are resolved before a wider audience of multiple domestic and international actors with different stakes and priorities. With multiple actors involved, the vectors of the conflict are not unidirectional, and even settlements entail multidimensional formulas.

The need for change in the state's conflict resolution role is paramount and, in many ways, essential if the Turkish polity is to perpetuate its ability to provide basic public goods such as security and stability. The currently held approach harms Turkish interests and deprives Turkey of the ability to solve its deep-rooted social and security problems. An alternative approach could involve, first, a change in the framing of conflicts away from a we-the-state versus them understanding; second, readiness to engage multiple actors pertaining to a conflict; third, getting professional assistance from academia and experts; and fourth, laying the groundwork for developing institutional capacity in conflict resolution. To that end, it would be wise for policy makers to work for the consolidation of democracy and to depend on the rule of law to set the stage for a more comprehensive political and cultural shift in state-led conflict resolution efforts in Turkey.

4

The Crisis in Turkey's Foreign and Security Policy

The failed coup on July 15, 2016, was a wake-up call indicating the urgent need for institutional reform in Turkey. The period after the failed coup not only pertains to the massive purges and changes in state cadres, but also signifies a broader need to consolidate state power in Turkey. This chapter analyzes attempts to redirect foreign policy in the context of the multiple crises after July 15, which are, more broadly, part of a larger state crisis in Turkey. The failed coup resulted not in a break with the past but in an attempt to fine-tune Turkish foreign policy) in response to the changing domestic landscape and international context.

Turkish foreign policy is a case in point of the growing mismatch between the ideas and worldviews of the political leadership and foreign policy practice under the strains of the state crisis. This mismatch has emerged as one of the driving factors in the quest for change in foreign policy in the post–Arab Spring era. The gap between the country's capabilities and resources and its regional and international commitments has overshadowed former success stories in Turkish foreign policy by conveying an all-encompassing sense of siege, retreat, and isolation. The liberal approach to foreign policy, despite the selective pragmatic flexibility of the

Parts of this chapter are reprinted with permission from Bülent Aras, "The Crisis and Change in Turkish Foreign Policy after July 15," *Alternatives: Global, Local, Political* 44, no. 1 (February 2019): 6–18. doi.org/10.1177/0304375419837415.

ruling Justice and Development Party (AKP) leadership, turned out to be unsustainable and, eventually, a hard sell for the public vis-à-vis burgeoning crises. Foreign policy became a battleground for domestic schisms nurtured also by increasing political polarization in the country. The political elite gradually lost track of earlier commitments and a sense of ownership regarding broad regional and international issues beyond those core issues they could manipulate to hold on to their domestic objectives. These elites also turned against each other while, paradoxically, trying to consolidate electoral support based on vital foreign policy issues such as Syria, Cyprus, the Kurdish question, and relations with Russia, the United States, and the West in general.

The half-baked plans to adjust foreign policy faced not only a deepening state crisis calling for an urgent change in the name of raison d'être, but also further erosion of human and material resources for such an endeavor in the context of prevalent domestic concerns. The failed coup engendered a unique opportunity for adjustment in foreign policy since postcoup national consensus held the potential to minimize opposition to institutional and policy reform. However, the hope for a consensual political atmosphere relinquished its place to a deepening state crisis in a short period of time that has been framed in a way to resuscitate enemy-threat perceptions among the Turkish public. In this sense, the postcoup state crisis narrative was what hegemonic actors made of it and was imposed on the opposition and the public at large. The ideational and conversational construction of the crisis was about "the mapping together of a great variety of disparate events unified through the identification of some common essence."[1] On that note, the failed coup was "intersubjectively interpreted as necessitating change."[2]

The post–July 15 narrative elevated the degree of legitimacy for what Charles Hermann[3] calls foreign policy makers' "self-correcting change" toward an alternative course of foreign policy. Recalibration in foreign policy emerged as a corrective political objective of the ruling party after July 15, even if mostly on a rhetorical basis. In addition, the atmosphere of uncertainty in the postcoup era created an opportunity for authoritative policy making, and this role was taken over by President Recep Tayyip Erdoğan to reflect his vision on Turkish foreign policy. Michael Barnett emphasizes that policy makers constantly seek "to guide political mobilization toward a particular outcome and for a particular goal by using symbols, metaphors, and cognitive cues to organize experience and fix meaning to events."[4] The new narrative and guided political mobilization by the AKP government in Turkey represented the redirection of foreign policy as a necessity of the emerging situation, not an offshoot of a sense of failure in the previous era.

Despite the new narrative and authoritative control of the implementation of foreign policy, presumed redirection or recalibration has proved unlikely to materialize in Turkish foreign policy in the post–July 15 era. The absence of a novel vision and readjusted foreign policy goals, the priority of domestic calculations over international concerns, the inability to bridge the gap between commitments and resources, among other concerns, substantiate this argument. The new narrative of living constantly in extraordinary conditions, and the need for survivalist strategies do not correspond with the requirements for capacity and institution building. Such narratives fail to address the endogenous nature of the broader crisis. Against this background, there is not a solid plan for change and reform in Turkish foreign policy at large, but only a rhetorical emphasis on such actions. Even worse, this complexity enabled the marginal nationalist and ultranationalist groups to hijack the rhetorical quest for alternative arrangements in Turkish foreign policy.

The Systemic Crisis

The change to a presidential system has eroded the regular functioning of parliamentary democracy without putting a well-defined and tested constitutional order in its place in Turkey. The new power structure has accelerated the ongoing and, to some extent, pending changes in the structure of foreign-policy making since the end of the Cold War. The main resistance to change was the hegemonic role of the military bureaucracy, which assumed subordinate roles to all other institutions in foreign and security policy. First, the traditional power houses, such as the National Security Council and the General Staff of the Military and Foreign Ministry, lost their previously influential positions and retained only some organizational, compiling, and bookkeeping roles. Second, foreign policy became an extended arm of partisan domestic politics for the purposes of bringing victories home to consolidate public support, which in turn led the opposition to amplify foreign policy losses. Thus the premise that foreign policy should be based on national interests has become a relic of the past. Third, diminishment of the roles of traditional institutions paved the way for the rise of personalities as the main determining factors of policy.

This radical shift is also a reflection of the blurring of boundaries between domestic politics and foreign policy, and the politicization of the latter. The past decade has arguably seen Abdullah Gül's foreign policy, Ahmet Davutoğlu's foreign policy, and above all, the overarching personal hold of Erdoğan's foreign policy. Although political leadership relies on the choices of the ruling party and its supporting clientele, personal preferences largely inform the government's policies and alignments in foreign policy.

The turn from institutions to a personalized foreign policy line further widened the burgeoning gap between ideas and capabilities in foreign policy for the sake of pursuing the political agenda of the AKP on the basis of the personal choices of its leadership. The early success of the AKP's foreign policy largely relied on the harmony of the Erdoğan-Gül duo, top personalities in party leadership, and their overall orientation toward Europeanization and their unprecedented initiatives of conflict resolution—for example, in Cyprus and Armenia—together with the consequential support of the pro-European elements in the bureaucracy for European Union (EU) integration.[5]

The quest for an ambitious policy in Turkey's wider neighborhood gained applause abroad but failed to be internalized and owned by the bureaucratic cadres. The new quest for grandeur forced the bureaucratic elite out of their comfort zone, inducing them to extend their portfolios to include conflict geographies in neighboring regions and even out-zone territories in Africa and Asia.[6] As one bureaucrat aptly put it: "The Turkish bureaucracy was ill-equipped to provide an expansionist or even a more conciliatory soft power role beyond its traditionalist concerns for security and stability."[7] In the Davutoğlu era—the period roughly between 2009 and 2015—Turkey sought foreign policy activism in regional and global issues, and thus undermined the traditional roles of the bureaucracy, if only by demonstrating its unpreparedness for such an active role.[8] Davutoğlu attempted "to bridge this gap by bringing together his team of experts and co-opted a selective cadre including the Foreign Ministry's top diplomats, which made a remarkable start but failed to build on preliminary efforts for outreach when the Arab revolts undermined the pillars of Turkey's regional policy."[9]

The Gül and Davutoğlu eras also represented a missed opportunity for capacity building to bridge the gap between ideas and capabilities in the Turkish foreign policy apparatus, which could have better engaged the regional conflicts and informed the limits of seeking grandeur in regional policy. This period was unique in terms of domestic stability and an international environment that provided opportune prospects for a new foreign policy orientation. The half-baked endeavors for capacity building left Turkey short of the necessary military, intelligence, academic, and linguistic networks, and alternative sources of power projection. Ideational depth without capacity ended up with an approach of a rhetorical and, in a way, a historicist-romantic understanding of Turkey's neighborhood.[10] Turkey's openings near and far have fallen short of the early euphoria. Despite more than 250 years of Westernization attempts, the Turkish presence and networks in Western circles have been limited and have proved unsustainable at a time of global restructuring. Turkey more and more sought an ideational link with its neighborhood in a complex international setting.

Overall, the capacity gap, with material and ideational components, created a transitional deficiency in foreign policy. Ideationally the inability to foster a foreign policy ethos among bureaucratic cadres in line with emerging foreign policy practice, and to have the bureaucracy assume a facilitating role in harmonizing a regional profile and relations with international powers such as the EU, the United States, Russia, and China, has proved a major setback.[11] While the bureaucracy stuck to the ambiguous Peace at Home, Peace in the World motto, which symbolized cautionary and status quoist leanings in traditional foreign policy practice, the AKP leadership aimed to raise the Turkish profile through regional initiatives and integration. Against the conventional bureaucratic line that upheld the idea that Turkish modernization was still incomplete and thus that the focus should be on domestic consolidation—for example, via the elimination of domestic threats—the AKP's foreign-policy thinking set sail beyond territorial boundaries.[12]

Two issues have proved consequential in defying the AKP's foreign policy approach. First, the lack of consensus on the validity of AKP's foreign policy approach in the context of the staying power of traditional doctrine that cherishes holding on to the status quo with a security-first outlook. Second, the absence of political ownership other than by the AKP, and growing criticism of Turkish handling of the Arab Spring and particularly the Syrian crisis, which paradoxically enmeshed the AKP leadership further in conflicts with the reasoning that they must prove others wrong.[13] Without bureaucratic inclusion of its principles, Davutoğlu's zero-problems policy[14] fell victim to institutional shortages and became dependent on success stories, which rendered it both transient and unable to introduce the necessary policy changes in the context of growing insecurity within and across Turkey's borders.

Yet beyond this divergence on principles and goals related to foreign policy, the ruling party failed to beef up its claim for a regional role in generating the required institutional capacity and governance networks. Apart from the development and aid projects of the Turkish Cooperation and Coordination Agency (TİKA), for regions from southeastern Europe to Africa and faraway Asian territories, as a soft-power projection tool, the cultural, intelligence, and diasporic components of the organizational structure of foreign policy largely remained intact. It was a bit shocking to learn that only after the coup attempt did the government accept the need to rehash the still-pending institutionalization of foreign intelligence, which was added to the prerogatives of the National Intelligence Organization (MIT) with a legislative change as late as April 2014.[15]

Yurtdışı Türkler, established to coordinate Turkish diaspora activities, and the Yunus Emre Institute, created to promote Turkish language and culture, following the steps of the British Council and the Cervantes Institute, did not succeed in evolving into active soft-power policy agencies and have been unable to cultivate a Turkey brand in target geographies in accordance with the ambitious foreign policy agenda.[16] In addition, though

Turkey's diplomatic missions reached a prominent level in terms of numbers,[17] in terms of staff, resources, and expertise they remained behind the requirements of Turkey's ambitious Africa, Asia, and Latin America openings. This capacity was further weakened by the high number of purges within the diplomatic cadres following July 15 failed coup. Although there is substantial progress in academic and civil society capacity through the opening of new faculties, institutes, think tanks and NGOs, the quantitative increase did not match with the needs of Turkish foreign policy, and their input remained marginal in the foreign-policy making process.

The humanitarian arena has been a realm of Turkish foreign policy in which policy makers performed far above average.[18] Turkey has become one of the top donor countries in global terms, has hosted the highest number of refugees, and has taken on the vital role of shock absorption vis-à-vis the Syrian humanitarian crisis, even though this role has become more and more fragile due to growing socioeconomic issues in Turkey.[19] Turkey's Red Crescent (Kızılay), the Disaster and Emergency Management Presidency (AFAD), and humanitarian NGOs have proved adept at responding to humanitarian crises across Turkey's borders and beyond. The Turkish education and health infrastructure has proved resilient enough to accommodate more than 3.5 million refugees. In addition, Turkey's humanitarian NGOs took independent initiative to help people facing humanitarian disasters in a widespread geography, from Somalia to Myanmar, and became the civilian arm of the Turkish version of "humanitarian diplomacy."[20]

Erdoğan has had an overarching personal role in Turkish foreign policy as the political leader of the AKP. Yet his willingness to delegate and consult has reached its limits, especially after the 2014 presidential elections amid growing security crises inside and across Turkey. This change not only meant the marginalization of the role played earlier by Davutoğlu, who served as the prime minister until May 2016 and still co-opted the foreign and security bureaucracy in decision making, but also increased the centralized role of the presidency and Erdoğan's entourage. Therefore, the foreign missions in Turkey more and more looked to the presidential palace in Beştepe, rather than to the foreign ministry in Balgat and the Genelkurmay in Kızılay to get hints about the course of Turkish foreign policy.

The earlier framework of foreign policy, which had been largely masterminded by Davutoğlu, came to be overshadowed by Erdoğan's personal decisions, even if it still formed the ideational basis of the latter's foreign policy choices. Thus the differentiation between Davutoğlu the politician and Davutoğlu the mentor was still valid. In any case, Davutoğlu's attempt to visit US president Barack Obama in Washington, DC, reportedly marked the end of Erdoğan's patience for the pseudo dual structure during the transition to the presidential system.[21] Erdoğan gave a message to the world that he had assumed the foreign policy portfolio from Davutoğlu and restored his role as the ultimate decision maker. His immediate move was to cultivate relationships with his counterparts by trying to deepen his existing ties and develop new ones.

Erdoğan's foreign policy has also been determined by a blurring of the boundaries between domestic and foreign policy. The change of his discourse from "conservative democracy"[22] to nationalist-conservatism throughout the years has found reflection inter alia in his foreign policy approach. Turkish foreign policy followed on Erdoğan's political agenda rather than a more institutional or doctrinal-ideational base. Thus Turkish foreign policy became a bargaining chip in his broader effort to consolidate the presidential system in Turkey. To that end, in addition to challenging Turkey's traditional partners, Erdoğan did not hesitate to develop single-item and largely transactional relationships with his foreign counterparts.[23] Erdoğan's personal perceptions have also become influential in Turkish foreign policy, as has been evident in his repudiation of the rule of Egyptian and Syrian leaders Abdel Fattah al-Sisi and Bashar al-Assad and his confrontation of the Saudi crown prince, while he has maintained close relations with the Russian, Iranian, and Qatari leaderships.

As with many countries in the region, the Arab Spring has been a turning point for Turkey. The positive change in Turkish foreign policy toward long-term peace, stability, and cooperation in the region before the Arab Spring was quickly and unexpectedly overturned by the uprisings into a process of securitization, partly as a result of Turkey's own domestic problems and problems developing in its backyard.[24] Since the 2014 presidential election, the symbolic presidential palace has become the mainstay for foreign relations as Erdoğan mustered a team of advisors and public relations and social media experts to undertake day-to-day formulation of policy guidelines. This selection has proved consequential in the adaptation to rhetorical animosity toward the West and regional rivals. The president also appointed his senior advisors as ambassadors without portfolio, which was construed as preparation for presidential appointment of noncareer ambassadors.[25] The presidential spokesperson arguably received a superior position in the political hierarchy and set the tone for foreign policy as the president's messenger in chief. This role was later partly assigned to the director of communications in the presidency, particularly in public diplomacy.[26]

As an extension of the presidency's outreach, yet another novelty has been the establishment of the AKP lobby and civil society organizations in foreign capitals, which not only transgressed the prerogatives of Turkish embassies in terms of representation, but also overreached via initiatives for social engineering of the diaspora in the context of anti-Turkey groupings.[27] The holding of elections abroad for the first time in the 2014 presidential elections also enlarged the AKP's political influence over the Turkish diaspora, especially in European countries. The AKP has opened four offices in Belgium, Northern Cyprus, the UK and Germany, and is planning to open five more in the US, Russia, France, Bosnia and Herzegovina, and Macedonia.[28]

Erdoğan's quest to steer a new course for Turkey has earned additional, though far from consensual, political legitimacy beyond his electoral mandate. This came on top of a virtual bureaucratic shutdown with massive purges in the bureaucracy and the near elimination of power brokers in the military-security apparatus. Therefore, the government-bureaucracy relationship is now a one-way relationship more than ever before. The government has appeared committed to appoint purely loyalist elements of the bureaucracy to top positions. In that sense, yielding to the government's predetermined policy choices has become the default mode, while formulating alternative scenarios and cost-benefit analyses has become risky for political survival. Overall, this symbiotic government-bureaucracy relationship has carried the risk of minimizing the effectiveness of policy making and undermining the government's ability to manage the growing internal and external crises.

Erdoğan's role in all aspects of the state, especially Turkish foreign policy, and as the de facto center of power in Ankara thus set out the building blocks of the presidential system. The approval of constitutional changes on April 16, 2017, was a major step toward the institutionalization of what has been dubbed as the "Turkish-type Presidential system."[29] However, even beyond the opposition's reluctance to accept the results of the referendum, the dual system of parliamentary regime and presidential authority over three organs of the government created centralized confusion in Ankara. While parliament still held the power to enact laws and seal the government's policies, Erdoğan's overarching personality rose above all limits of legality-institutional checks and separation of powers, becoming a defining element in the Turkish constitutional regime. The abnormality was that while the parliamentary system was largely upheld up until the June 2018 elections, with the cabinet members approved and supervised by the parliament, presidential decisions were kept outside the supervision of the legislative organ. This situation not only undermined the basics of the parliamentary system but also put the AKP politicians in the uncomfortable situation of defending Erdoğan's foreign policy practices before the parliament, even when the president infringed on the political prerogatives of their respective governments.

The June 24, 2018, presidential and parliamentary elections have proved a new landmark in the transition to the presidential system. Having defied the remnants of electoral opposition to the AKP's rule, Erdoğan believed that, perhaps more than ever before, he had a mandate to steer a self-designed course for the Turkish government. This was expeditiously reflected in the post–June 24 bureaucratic restructuring. First, Erdoğan minimized the political and institutional authority of the ministries. Government ministers turned into appointed technocrats, lacking the political mandate of parliamentary representation. Four ministers who were elected for parliamentary seats; namely, the ministers of Foreign Affairs, Interior, Finance, and Justice, had to abandon their seats in accord with the constitutional arrangement to separate presidential authority from parliamentary oversight.

Second, the presidential palace was transformed into the epicenter of policy making, with new councils and offices. For example, the Security and Foreign Policies Council was earmarked to formulate alternative policies and carry out coordination with stakeholders, including the ministries, civil society organizations, and experts. Even though the president and members of the council were appointed only as late November 2018,[30] it is quintessentially designed to function in a manner similar to the National Security Council in the US presidential system. The military was assigned a relatively subservient role in the new bureaucratic structure of security and foreign policy making and has been placed under the mandate of the Ministry of National Defense in the presidential cabinet.

Third, the president used his ultimate and peculiar authority to appoint top bureaucrats. His appointment of a high number of noncareer ambassadors to top-priority posts like the United States, Japan, China, Indonesia, and the Netherlands signals the transition to bureaucratic governance of foreign policy according to the president's political and managerial priorities. The foreign ministry now has three deputy ministers, one replacing the traditional political director–undersecretary; the second assuming the tasks of the former undersecretary of the EU ministry, which was integrated into the Ministry of Foreign Affairs; and a third assuming financial and administrative tasks. The appointments are indicative of the way ahead, with the first two ministers appointed from among career diplomats and the third being a former political advisor to the minister. In this sense, while the day-to-day functioning of foreign policy is still left in the hands of career bureaucrats, the future design and path of foreign policy will now be administered by AKP political cadres.

The Political Crisis

In Turkish politics, as well as in comparable political systems, the governing party is made up of a coalition of competing political allegiances. Erdoğan's individual hold on power within the party ranks has been a product of political exigency, not a cast process developed in foreseen stages. Erdoğan might owe his power to fighting back the resistance of the bureaucratic and oligarchic elements in the state system, yet he has also been able to steer clear of them thanks to coalition building inside and beyond party dynamics.[31] Occasionally he has used relations with the

Table 3
AKP Alliances and Foreign Policy

Date	Alliances	Foreign Policy Orientation
2002–10	AKP–liberal groups	EU and the West
2008–12	AKP-Gülenists	EU and the West, new openings in Africa, Asia, and Latin America
2014–	AKP-MHP-Ulusalcılar (ultranationalists)	Eurasia, Russia, and China

EU and the United States, and has co-opted liberal intellectuals and even the Gülenists to tame the bureaucratic leviathan. Beyond these external elements outside the party ranks, Erdoğan had the backing of co-opted Erbakanists-Islamists (Milli Görüşçüler), Europeanists, statists, nationalists, Kurds, and neoliberalists within the AKP, who were generally supportive of Turkey's global economic integration, with different degrees of embrace of the country's defining Turkish-Islamic identity.

This whole coalition is now a relic of the past. Erdoğan seemingly has absolute control in the party and over the political system in Turkey. He has been able to marginalize the opposition, defy alternative levers of power, and isolate possible contenders for leadership within the party ranks after effectively dividing them through co-optation or sidelining. He rules over a regime that has democratic legitimacy thanks to mass electoral appeal but is far from inclusive and consensual due to minimal integration of competing interests of class, religion, ethnicity, or ideology. The resultant operating system is dependent on Erdoğan alone and lacks ideological consistency and balancing factors amid policy failures.

Erdoğan's capacity to address critical issues of Turkish politics such as the Kurdish question and Turkish nationalism is one of the reasons for his ability to protect his peak position in Turkish politics. Despite the fact that these issues have not been at the top of the AKP's agenda, he saw no harm or risk in putting them on the agenda when he considered it to be necessary. He took unprecedented steps in owning these issues and was able to gain more Kurdish votes than even the People's Democratic Party (HDP) as the pro-Kurdish party.[32] When the tide turned, he was quick to abandon the Kurdish question and embraced Turkish nationalist and statist concerns for identity and security. This pragmatic twist inter alia sowed the seeds for the AKP-Nationalist Action Party (MHP) alliance by securitizing Turkish politics to prevent Kurdish separatist groups from maneuvering and by reclassifying the political framework according to presidential terms in order to install Turkish-Islamic exceptionalism as a conclusive ethos in the new coalition.

Erdoğan has been largely criticized lately, particularly in Western circles, for dragging Turkey toward authoritarianism. However, that does not negate the fact that the AKP leader has possessed the capacity to set a conservative-nationalist alliance that has sustained vital electoral support for his domestic and foreign policies. His majoritarian comprehension of politics has enabled him to lead in molding the requests and worries of the public majority, which has proved consequential for upholding the AKP's status as the owner of and campaigner for Muslim grievances. Beyond these short-term dynamics, however, Erdoğan's political legacy will to a large extent rely on how he can sustain this grand coalition of conservative-nationalists in Turkish politics without alienating the minority groups that make up another fragmented half of society in total, such as the secularists, Kurds, Alevis, and estranged professionals.[33]

In their current form, Turkish politics under Erdoğan provides two alternatives for political competition: either loyalty and resignation inside the governing party, or protest, rebuff, and recently reinvigorated calls for resistance from the opposition.[34] Thus political stability depends on either integrating the opposition's concerns or, with a short-termist outlook, their exclusion. This tactical approach seems to have worked until the March 2019 mayoral elections, setting a barrier between the discontented in the AKP and conservative circles, and moderate elements in the opposition.

Polarization is further deepened by that binary dynamic in Turkish politics and also shapes Turkey's foreign policy discourse. Since the boundaries between domestic and foreign policy have become blurred more than ever, foreign policy has increasingly turned into an extension of domestic policy, and any criticism is rebuffed as a renouncement of national interests, authoritatively defined by the government. Western passivity in response to the failed coup made the Turkish government and public feel isolated and created resentment. Government circles, in need of a rhetorical strategy in keeping with the partly self-constructed siege mentality, hastily espoused the third-worldist and anti-imperialist discourse of the ultranationalist elements. Paradoxically, the AKP government came to concurrently hold on to Davutoğlu's policy premises, such as regional leadership and ownership, only this time with the counterbalancing rhetorical base of anti-Westernism and Turkish nationalism.

This blend might have been a product of the perceived yet undocumented Russian hand in misinformation, propaganda, and news manipulation in Turkey.[35] Moreover, pro-Russian and anti-American circles manipulated Turkish anger over US support for the Gülenists and groups affiliated with the Kurdistan Workers' Party (PKK) in Syria to agitate the sense of abandonment by the Western alliance. While the government aspired to keep conservative and nationalist elements en bloc, it has been unable to take notice of the discursive turn toward anti-Westernism and Turkish isolation from its traditional partners. Therefore, the S-400 crisis and US reactions appeared to be a surprise to many policy makers in Ankara.[36]

The opposition's reaction to that contradictory drift has been to it to prove their self-fulling prophecy of Islamists' aversion to democracy. However, the opposition parties also seemed far from able to offer convincing arguments about Turkey's long-term alignment to ward off the conflictual cycle.[37] All in all, the minimization of support from Turkey's traditional partners and its overall external isolation further reinforced the Turkish government's need for foreign policy success stories to be used for domestic consumption, which again fed into the vicious circle of isolation, repudiation, and alienation in Turkish foreign policy.

In general the tipping point between domestic politics and foreign policy has been the Turkish government's Syria policy, which has had divisive spillover effects. Erdoğan's unwavering support for the Syrian opposition and categorical rejection of the Assad regime has caused a major rift between the government and the opposition. While the former defended the Syria policy in humanitarian and geostrategic terms, the latter labeled it as sectarian and expansionist. Within this framework, the government has tapped into Islamic-nationalist concerns about the marginalization of Sunni interests in Syria and Iraq, as well as the Kurdish march toward autonomy and independence. The opposition, in turn, has emphasized that the growing security crisis is the result of the AKP's foreign policy and serves the ruling party's religious and sectarian agenda.[38] Overall, the divergent if not divisive visions on Turkish foreign policy have undermined efforts to ensure security and stability inside and beyond its borders, which has further fed into multiple crises in Turkish foreign policy.

The populist and more remarkably insular turn in Turkish politics, in accord with global trends, has undermined Turkey's broader efforts to mend fences. First, the government-controlled media and social media channels have produced an uncalculated and concurrently anti-American, -EU, -British, -Chinese, -German, -Iranian, -Israeli, and -Arab rhetoric for domestic consumption, which has left scant room for the desired reset in foreign relations. Turkey's earlier claim to rise above extant schisms in regional and global politics has given way to staying out of hegemonic regional and global coalitions and, hence, overall isolation. There is an urgent need for nuanced diplomacy, coalition building, and toning down of antagonistic rhetoric that makes international headlines daily.[39] Second, there is also a need for bipartisan consensus for weathering the multiple crises in foreign policy. The divisive nature of post–Arab Spring geopolitics undermined the delicate balances in Turkish politics. Therefore, it is necessary to take into consideration the present secular-pious, Kurdish-Turkish, and Alevi-Sunni cleavages in Turkish politics when addressing complex geopolitical challenges. Finally, Turkey's quest for recalibration carries the risk of being construed as capitulation and a U-turn, which again calls for broader domestic dialogue in policy making to ensure long-term follow-up regarding national interests.

The government occasionally hints at its readiness for cooperative arrangements with all possible partners, yet the fine-tuning between rhetoric and policy has largely been lost. This, in turn, has given a further boost to mutual mistrust with Western and regional countries. Despite a pretense for catching a tune with Doha and Moscow, and to a lesser extent with Tehran, Turkish regional policy is under duress from all directions and requires a broader recalibration. The Yıldırım government, which replaced Davutoğlu in May 2016, appeared hopeful of recalibration, with a seemingly pragmatic understanding of foreign policy under the motto of minimizing the number of enemies and maximizing the number of friends. While at face value this did not sound much different from the zero-problems approach, it aspired to narrow Turkey's conflict map, especially in relation to Israel, Russia, Syria, and Iraq. There was an implicit element of renunciation of the Davutoğlu era in terms of being pro-American and pro-European and, by implication, acting against Turkey's national and regional interests—hence the repudiation of the controversial decision to hit the Russian jet on the Turkish-Syrian border. It was a quest for denouncing the Davutoğlu era as a whole in the ensuing efforts to achieve regime consolidation in coalition with the nationalist MHP and implicitly the ultranationalist elements in the establishment.[40]

While Prime Minister Binali Yıldırım might not have opted for an anti-Western course in the beginning, the failed coup and the inability to garner concrete support for Turkey's cross-border operations in Syria and Iraq inevitably gave way to a rhetorical escalation, particularly against Washington, Berlin, and Brussels (both NATO and the EU). The progovernment papers and social media agents epitomized assumedly anti-imperialist discourse in order to vindicate the government's postcoup diplomacy. Alienating Western allies, the new government had to settle for reinvigorated ties with Russia, which also reflected the ideological preferences of the tacit AKP-MHP and arguably and tacitly the ultranationalist (*ulusalcılar*) coalition at home.[41] One of the policy implications of Turkey's growing isolation from the West was seeking Russian security guarantees for Turkish cross-border operations against PKK targets and respect for Turkish interests in northern Syria in return for a negotiated truce in Aleppo and subsequently in Idlib. Turkey also needed Russia's tacit approval to push the People's Protection Units (YPG) back and block further mass migration to Turkey in the context of the Assad regime's incursions in Idlib.

Turkey's geopolitics is both its most formidable asset and its biggest liability. It assigns Turkey a role broader than its political and economic capacity, and it overburdens its capacity to cope with complex and multidimensional conflicts. The Arab Spring overturned the Turkish role of interconnector between the West and the Islamic Middle East. Turkey not only became an intersection point and victim of the East-West conflict, but also came to face the severance of its ideational link to both worlds, which set the stage for a reincarnation of the historical solitude complex. It was unable to lead change especially in neighboring Syria, and its security concerns were elevated with expansion of the twin threats of PKK separatism and Daesh jihadism. Worse still, Turkey lost common ground with Arab partners, with the minor exception of Qatar, over major discord on the role of the Muslim Brotherhood in Arab politics, which left Turkish pro-Sunni tendencies devoid of major support. Turkish fixation on the overthrow of Egyptian president Mohamed Morsi and rejection of his successor, President Sisi, pushed the door wide open for anti-Turkish coalitions between Egypt, Greece, Cyprus, and—with a veiled role from behind the scenes—Israel in the eastern Mediterranean.[42] The United Arab Emirates and, to a lesser extent, Saudi Arabia also occasionally volunteered to disrupt Turkish interests.[43]

In retrospect, following the erosion of an active and soft-power approach in Turkish foreign policy, Turkey was left with no choice but to become more and more insular, primarily for self-protection against heightened security risks. Changing geostrategic equations played a major role. First, Russian and Iranian interventionism rolled back Turkey's largely self-assigned leadership claim in the Syrian transition. Second, the Obama administration's (and the subsequent Trump administration's) wobbling stance toward regional crises undermined an assumed Turkish-American and partly EU cooperation to steer the region toward normalization. Third, the prevalence of sectarian dynamics, fanned by the Saudi-Iranian rivalry, bogged down Turkish designs, more precisely pretensions of an all-embracing outreach to bring together moderate Sunnis and Shias.[44] Fourth, the changing dynamics of Arab geopolitics put Turkey on a collision course with pro-Western Sunni powers—that is, the Gulf monarchies (with the minor exception of Qatar), Egypt, and to a lesser extent Jordan, who were apprehensive about Turkish support for political Islam and the Muslim Brotherhood.[45] As a result, Turkey found itself embroiled in immediate multifrontal confrontation against Kurdish, Russian, Iranian,

Western, and Arab interests, in addition to structural discord with Israel, Iraq, Syria, Armenia, and Greece in its broader neighborhood.

Therefore, Turkey was not left with many options besides moving toward rapprochement with Russia to hedge against its growing isolation. How far an emerging Turkish-Russian partnership could serve the Turkish case for regional security and conflict resolution—from Syria to Cyprus, Armenia, and Ukraine—remains an open question. In theory, the Russian mastery of prospering in frozen conflicts contradicts the Turkish need for regional stability in order to maintain both internal political balance and economic growth. Yet in practice the two countries have proved adept at cooperating in the context of the destabilizing effects of the Syrian spillover and at joining forces to ameliorate the exclusionary policies of the West, particularly the United States. In any case, Turkish overtures to Russia are likely to undermine the Turkish alliance with the West and the United States in particular, especially with regard to the controversial issue of the sale of Russian S-400 ballistic missiles to Turkey.[46]

Against this backdrop, Turkish security concerns came to trump regional policy goals, such as support for like-minded regimes, with single focus on confronting the PKK's expansionism in Syria and Iraq. This lately brought Turkey and Iran together against Kurdish aspirations, particularly in Iraq. It also pushed Turkey into Russia's orbit to gain a free hand against PKK offshoots under the pretext of upholding Syrian territorial integrity. Thus Turkey seemed to have narrowed its external focus to an extension of the major domestic goal of fighting against PKK terrorism.

Beyond the flux in international dynamics, especially with the loss of direction in US politics and the EU, as well as the growing confidence of rising great powers such as China and Russia, Turkey appeared desperate to seek international support for regime consolidation after the coup attempt. This exclusively domestic focus hindered a possible Turkish role in meeting its security interests and balancing Western ties with broader global engagement. Turkey could have overcome a legitimate but narrow preoccupation with the PKK to lead the broader fight against terrorism in Syria and Iraq, which would have strengthened its hand in global equations. Rather Turkey turned itself into a rejectionist power, even if for certain legitimate reasons, opposing Russian and Iranian alliance with Assad, American alliance with the PYD, the Kurdistan Regional Government's independence referendum in Iraq, and the Arab-Israeli coalition against Iran. Thus Turkey pushed itself to the sidelines and ultimately did a disservice to its national interests.

Indeed, following a Hobbesian approach to counter all opposition, Ankara has at times adopted a more conciliatory approach toward the United States and the EU following an earlier rapprochement with Russia in Syria. Turkey's handling of crises after June 2018 presidential elections has been visibly more nuanced, especially given the fact that Ankara managed to stay relatively out of trouble and gained diplomatic ground in Idlib, the Pastor Andrew Brunson crisis, the Khashoggi murder, and the quadrilateral meeting with Germany, France, and Russia on Syria in İstanbul in 2018. Overall there has been a will for fence-mending, surely led by Erdoğan, to create ample room for maneuvering against the burgeoning economic and political downturn of his embattled presidency for the past five years.

Yet this attempt to transition into moderating the gloomy crisis mode faces the challenging task of accommodating the new AKP-MHP coalitional dynamics. Above all, Erdoğan's will to get rid of checks on his power now contradicts the need for co-opting the ultranationalist and insular worldview of its coalition partner. The MHP's statist background and ingrained advocacy for a security-first outlook in foreign policy is likely to undermine the government's need to recalibrate foreign policy. Overall, the government's balance sheet since the July 2016 coup attempt is a testament to this foresight. Despite the large-scale erosion of the bureaucratic cadres after the purges, the government chose to conduct a three-pronged war against terrorism beyond the conventional fight against the PKK and the Islamic State (ISIS) in Turkey, Syria, and Iraq. The postmodern fight against the Gülenists has put much strain on the government's capacity in intelligence, security, law, finance, and foreign relations. The end result of this large-scale fight, coupled with domestic polarization, has been Turkish involvement in and confrontation of a broad range of sources of instability. Although the military and security services seemingly operate under the government's control, further entanglement in conflicts might aggravate the systemic and political crises of transition in Turkey and risk further militarization of foreign policy, which would, in turn, further increase the role of the MHP and affiliated groups in Turkish politics.

Conclusion

The July 15 failed coup has aggravated the side effects of a systemic and political transition under the strains of state crisis on foreign-policy making in Turkey. Turkish foreign policy was already due for a process of reset and recalibration because of policy failures in the previous period. The systemic and political crises perpetuated in its aftermath created further obstacles for reset in the foreign-policy-making process, consolidated personal and partisan prerogatives in foreign policy, narrowed room for maneuver in regional and international policy, and imposed inconsistent policy agendas on the bureaucracy. With mixed signals for a broader realignment or even disalignment, Turkish foreign policy is more and more defined by hard power in regional policy, Eurasianist policy premises, accord and even bandwagoning with Russia, and concurrent moves to mend ties with the United States and the EU. The reason for this hybrid, even hodgepodge approach is the government's aversion to dealing with the root causes of the systemic and political crises intrinsic to institutional setup and capacity building in foreign policy. Rather than attempting a long-term and well-planned response, the government has tried to initiate change through a hegemonic political narrative and coercive use of state power. A consensual approach in the context of the failed coup could have minimized the impact of political and systemic crises via a possible initiative to reform the state apparatus and foreign and security policy as well. Yet corrective mechanisms are far from operational, while the government tries to save the day by playing on the fear of further insecurity and instability.

The painful process of switching from a parliamentary to a presidential system further debilitated the eroding institutional capacity of the foreign policy apparatus. Not only the complex security environment surrounding Turkey, but also the systemic and political crises blurring the line between domestic and foreign policy agendas played their part. As a continuation of these problems, the aggravation of security conditions resuscitated the statist reflex of defying the opposition and securitizing all relevant political issues. Consequently, "the rising concern of protecting territorial sovereignty has resulted in a psychology of constant state of emergency in the domestic arena and militarization in regional policy."[47]

This chapter analyzes an ongoing state crisis as the ruling party struggles to recalibrate foreign policy and to reform the institutional setup in foreign-policy making. Challenges in the neighborhood and the ongoing fight against transnational terrorist and anti-Turkey groupings require immediate action. Given that neither the systemic and political crises at home nor the security and geostrategic crises abroad are likely to disappear soon, there is a need to rise above short-termism and introduce institutional and capacity-building responses in Turkish foreign policy. The challenges extending from domestic politics to the region and vice versa necessitate comprehensive, conciliatory, and transformative policies. The most pressing issues reflective of these crises are generating capacity, building institutions, and improving coordination among traditional and new agencies of foreign policy structure. There is an urgent call for serious planning and thinking on how to reset and recalibrate foreign policy with a congruous set of grand narrative, principles, and goals of a new policy line.

Deep-running polarization and fragmentation run the risk of further derailing half-hearted endeavors for normalization in the domestic landscape, as well as for rerouting and recalibration of the foreign policy apparatus and the state structure at large. The failed coup was a direct corollary of the weak state, which was surfaced with visible fragility and vulnerability, even preceding massive purges and uncertainty, in the state-bureaucracy relationship. As argued elsewhere, "search for systemic change, state building, dealing with multiple security threats, economic stability, and development would depend on all-encompassing, inclusive, and participatory political processes in the country."[48]

In an ideal political environment wherein systemic and political crises were put at ease, the search for reset and restructuring in foreign policy would have been less challenging for the policy makers. The task is to protect vital national interests in a deteriorating security situation in the neighborhood, and to protect previous international openings in an era of global turmoil. If this would not be the case, half-hearted and short-term measures, accompanied by partisan attitudes, under the duress of political and systemic crises in a wider context of state crisis would be the cause of broader failures in Turkish foreign policy in the period ahead.

5

Reforming Turkey

The Way Forward

Turkey's most recent state crisis once again underscored the need for reform within the state apparatus and political system. Despite a number of attempts in the modern history of Turkey, the political elites have been restricted in their reform attempts mainly due to their weakness in the context of the state tradition and bureaucracy in Turkey. The Justice and Development Party (AKP) under Recep Tayyip Erdoğan has had a number of opportunities to rewrite the constitution, redesign the political system, and restructure the state system, especially in the aftermath of the July 15, 2016, coup attempt. The AKP's contradictory goals to both reform and dominate the system not only dismantled the fundamentals of the state apparatus but also further damaged the already weak institutions in Turkey. Subsequent blows to the judiciary and the military, on top of extraordinary executive powers under the state of emergency and the referendum on the presidential system, put Erdoğan in a superior position to redesign the state and politics in Turkey.

Erdoğan appeared ready to work through the system, but his premiership was not free from interruption and similar threats of nonelectoral intrusion on the system. In 2007 Erdoğan's response to the presidential crisis playing out in the parliament was to put to referendum the issue of the popular election of the president. The parliament voted to give him a seven-year respite to introduce an executive presidency. Yet the presidential system he might have hoped to lead was quite different from the one he actually succeeded in implementing in 2014.

The Turkey of 2014 was fundamentally different from the Turkey of 2007. First, Erdoğan had gained an uncontested upper hand in Turkish politics and had enlarged his majoritarian support. Second, the bureaucratic apparatus was cracking under the secularist-Gülenist rivalry. The secularists were dealt a heavy blow through Gülenist-led and government-supported court cases, which amounted to a widespread purge in the high levels of the secularist bureaucracy. Yet co-opting the Gülenists to shackle the bureaucratic leviathan came with a price, which eventually undermined Erdoğan's domestic and international reputation. Third, Turkey failed in its attempt to lead democratic and popular revolutions in the Middle East, from Libya to Egypt and Syria. Fourth, the succession crisis in the post-Erdoğan AKP brought Ahmet Davutoğlu to power but catapulted new schisms in government and the AKP to the forefront.

Erdoğan thus presented the systemic transition as a panacea to the burgeoning state crisis and defended his design of a sui generis, Turkish-type presidential system, which was supposed to not only put a final nail in the coffin of bureaucratic tutelage but also establish a managerial, efficient, and performance-based state administration. Despite high hopes for a smooth transition, though, Erdoğan faced two major problems with his goal of remaking the state in his own image: First, with his style of confrontational politics, he turned the issue of a presidential system into a vote on himself. He presented his political agenda as the embodiment of national interests and those opposing his agenda as adversaries, if not enemies, of the nation. Thereafter, the transition itself and the debate and referenda on the transition became exclusively an issue of supporting or opposing Erdoğan.

In 2014, when the first public presidential elections were held, Erdoğan was effectively against all other parties, and his popularity proved enough to beat them all. Yet things were to change with the succession crisis in the AKP; namely, the Erdoğan-Davutoğlu/Abdullah Gül schisms and the opposition's consolidation with the unwinding of the Kurdish reconciliation talks. Thus after the November 2015 elections, and with the prevalence of the security-first outlook, the Nationalist Action Party (MHP) became the AKP's coalition partner. While Erdoğan became more and more dominant over the state apparatus and the party, he was losing his support base among urbanites, professionals, secular liberals, Kurds, and even alternative power centers within the AKP. The end result was that the AKP turned into an instrument of Erdoğan's personal agenda, while Erdoğan became more dependent on the support of the MHP to deliver electoral victories for the transition. The AKP won the April 2017 constitutional referendum and the June 2018 presidential elections by a narrow margin, even with the MHP's vital support. Remarkably, Erdoğan's electoral fights for survival got almost no support from his former allies, such as former president Gül, former prime minister Davutoğlu, and former deputy prime minister Ali Babacan.

The second problem with Erdoğan's goal of remaking the state in his own image was that his scorched-earth tactics crowded out the AKP's ability to lay the groundwork for a suitable succession. Fighting several battles on highly volatile ground, from the geostrategic map of the post–Arab Spring Middle East to fighting the Kurdistan Workers' Party (PKK), Daesh, the Gülenists, and others, left scant room for preparing a politically and institutionally feasible constitutional transition. Despite a broad-based longing for a new and civilian constitution since 1982, Turkey was unable to articulate this change. In the 2011 elections the AKP's foremost electoral promise was to finalize cross-party efforts to put an end to the militarily designed constitutional order. Failing to find common ground with other parties, the AKP first tried monopolizing the political system through elections, and in the end used the post–July 15 atmosphere to introduce a haphazard constitutional order. The lack of erudition had to do with the purges in the bureaucracy and academia but also, above all, Erdoğan's choice to tailor a new system to fit his personal agenda.

In any case, this final attempt discontinued the earlier quest for parliamentary and judicial autonomy, an executive-led system with entrenched checks and balances, protection of basic rights, and demystification of the state and the statist hold on Turkish society. The state structure, designed mostly by presidential decrees, created confusion within the state apparatus, sidelined the permanent bureaucracy, diminished efficiency, complicated decision-making processes, monopolized policy making, and used political appointments in the bureaucracy as a means of control and clientelism. It failed to arrange a hierarchical order, and it generated overlapping and conflicting roles within and between different offices and ministries. Subsequent attempts to repair the institutional gaps and dysfunctional state apparatus turned the overall exercise into a confusing puzzle of trial and error.

Therefore, it would not be going too far to conclude that the transition to the presidential system in Turkey did not satisfy the long-awaited need for reform. On the contrary, it created extended areas of conflict that necessitated conciliatory reform to address the acute state crisis. In 2015 Turkey was facing a major security crisis, which rendered political campaigns, urban life, and tourism insecure. Unprecedentedly, people were concerned about life outdoors in major urban settings, such as İstanbul and Ankara. This gave rise to a sustained and resolute fight against forces of instability. Turkey restored security and conducted operations inside and outside Turkey to incapacitate the PKK, Daesh, and the Gülenists, which have played major roles in destabilizing the security order in the country. Yet the price tag of this fight has been prolongation of the state of emergency and its practice afterward; all-out criminalization of the opposition, civil society, and intellectuals; mass purges in the bureaucracy and, most important, the judiciary; politicization of judicial cases; loss of trust in society; and intrusions on the free-market economy and property rights. These developments unwound the AKP's almost two decades–long case for civilizing politics and for extending freedoms and rights.

Against this backdrop of state, systemic, political, and foreign policy crises, reform is urgent. The absence of responsive, conciliatory, and consequential reform would mean the deepening of these crises and, even more important, further deinstitutionalization and loss of state capacity and political legitimacy. The current state structure, which has been unable to deliver efficiency and performance, surely needs to be overhauled. Even government circles have conceded this fact and are in the process of making certain amendments.[1] The following sections bring forth ideas about how to address the issue of state reform, and how to deal with deficits in state conflict resolution roles and reset foreign and security policy in Turkey.

Reforming Institutions

The World Bank reported that "being realistic about what is politically and institutionally feasible" is one of the foremost determinants in public sector reform.[2] In Turkey, too, the reform and restructuring process requires cooperation and a level of understanding between the government, public opinion, and the bureaucracy. Polarization and disenfranchisement are recipes for further fragmentation in Turkish politics. Fighting in an all-or-nothing approach to eliminate the bureaucracy either dilapidates state authority or engenders political instability if the bureaucracy proves astute enough to turn the crisis in its favor. Therefore, the current state crisis, further aggravated by the growing political and foreign policy crises in Turkey, drives a wedge between the case for majoritarian decision making and the ultimate goal of political transition.

In theory the AKP government has set the ultimate goal of transforming the Turkish state from an administrative state into a managerial state. Despite the creation of an administrative structure and appointments to bureaucratic and political offices, there appears to be confusion among the government cadres about setting a particular course. Reading between the lines, Erdoğan's political appointments of high-level bureaucrats who would, in theory, facilitate the implementation of government policies faces the question of human resources. The AKP does not have a pool of professionals to replace bureaucratic expertise; nor has it developed capacity-building tools such as training and education, goals and benchmarks for performance, objective criteria for selection and promotion, delegation of duties, division of labor, or coordination between agencies.

The state apparatus is already sounding the SOS over the effective practice of putting the cart before the horse. As was conceded in AKP circles, the presidential system minimizes the role of parliament and parliamentarians.[3] Moreover, the bureaucratic structure, which used to depend on political mandate, now depends on presidential choices, technocratic leanings of the nonparliamentarian ministers, and the short-termist considerations of political appointees. The abolition of undersecretaries and their replacement by a system of deputy ministers produced at best a dysfunctional copy of the old system. While the permanent bureaucratic cadres strive to perpetuate their good old institutional reflexes, as certain former undersecretaries were appointed as deputy ministers, new political appointees strive to learn about bureaucratic culture and figure out their way between the presidency's expectations and the eroding institutional capacities of the ministries and agencies.

Even if the current approach of creative destruction might be seen as a measure to curb bureaucratic resistance and optimize public sector performance, such an overly optimist perspective seems to have underestimated the potential pitfalls ahead. First, the long history of patrimonial tradition and state hegemony vis-à-vis all societal actors in Turkey would form the background of resistance to even well-thought-out and conciliatory reform. On that note, bureaucratic institutions' resistance to change would in any case make the assumed transition a challenging task, while the current approach makes it almost impossible to co-opt the reformist sections in bureaucracy.

Second, a major mistake was made on the sequence of public sector and constitutional reforms. Without defining the constitutional specifics of the presidential system through legislation, the government's move to transform the bureaucracy gave way to legitimacy issues and further confusion. Presently the bureaucratic structures are losing consistency and are struggling to find a feasible direction in terms of human resources policies, administrative and financial arrangements, and institutional ethos. The latter took an especially significant hit, given that certain groups and personalities in the bureaucracy used the confusion to their advantage, which gave rise to nepotism, favoritism, corruption, and arbitrary implementation of laws and regulations. Subjectivism and nepotism are diseases that the prospective reform processes should decisively address to restore trust and professionalism among the state cadres.

Third, the reform process is unlikely to move in a linear fashion, and thus will beget step-by-step frictions and compromises. The specifics of the reform agenda, yet to be disclosed as of April 2020, would engender pros and cons and would have to be implemented in the context of political uncertainty in Turkey.

Finally, changing the entrenched bureaucratic culture is a gigantic task that requires astute leadership and well-thought-out reform designs to move forward. The April 2017 referendum was expected to usher in an era of administrative reform in accord with the proponents of the presidential system's self-assigned orientation toward governmental efficiency. What transpired in its aftermath was the state of emergency, with unchecked executive decrees. Even worse, the dichotomy between the constitutional order and executive practice, as well as evasion of the propensity for reform has publicly eroded the government's commitment to state reform. Instead, a rough image of the president's full control over all three organs of the state and bureaucracy, along with the fusion of the public and private sectors in an evolving corporatist fashion, overshadow the broader need for further public sector reform.

After the constitutional amendments, the assumed quest to melt all state organs and sectors under the presidential administrative structure did not yield to managerialism and governmental efficiency, let alone responsiveness, accountability, and transparency. Thus it nurtured further insecurity and mistrust within the state apparatus. The bureaucracy was uncertain about its prospects and thus used its ultimate tool, namely stalling tactics and reserving its administrative expertise, to oppose the government's agenda. The current picture of political and economic mismanagement only discredits the government and its projections for state reform.

To break this mismatch between political rhetoric and practice, presidential rule needs to introduce consensual dialogue for reform and begin introducing practical steps, starting from the easiest (recruitment and setting benchmarks) to the hardest (changing bureaucratic culture and ethos). Reform in public administration requires substance and details in addition to public demand and the political will to pursue reform goals. There is no one-size-fits-all formula, and each bureau has its own specifics. Functional peculiarities determine the change in the bureau, ranging from the degree of autonomy to structural design.

Therefore, a feasible preliminary course would build on broader demands for good governance, responsive and transparent public administration, and general commitment to better services rendered, as well as the overall functioning of the state apparatus, including recruitment, pay, and promotions. In general, administrative reform, institution building, and capacity development require at least some degree of will and participation from different bureaus in the state apparatus. Selective engagement with political principles would help but would not ensure ultimate success. Again, the determinant of public policy success is defining objective performance criteria, establishing a normative order for hiring and firing, setting benchmarks for policy implementation, and harmonization between the government's policy agenda and that of the current bureaucracy's vested interests (related to promotions, for example), as well as the assumption of prospective roles under the new system. The process of transformation would be smoother in a plural and democratic political atmosphere.[4]

Currently the public sector needs an immediate resupply of human and material resources to compensate for the purges. This is both a chance to achieve and a hurdle before the reform agenda. There should be substantial change in the recruitment of civil servants. The criteria for recruitment and promotion should be talent, expertise, merit, and to a degree, equal representation of subgroups in society, above all women. Turkey's leadership should also pursue possibilities for public-private partnership to avail itself of the established successes of the private sector in the management of the bureaucracy. Good governance might sound cliché, but it still offers the best route for national reconciliation and institution building. Capacity building entails, inter alia, education, training, and legitimate policy goals. The first two of these necessitate institutionalization, the latter democratic legitimacy.

Reforming the State's Conflict Resolution Roles

Bureaucratic quality refers to the strength of administrative and infrastructural capacity. According to Cullen Hendrix, it captures three of the most important components of state capacity: "Professionalism, insulation from political pressure, and efficacy in delivering government services."[5] The bureaucratic apparatus in Turkey is more and more required to rethink and seek high-quality, creative solutions for the ongoing domestic and foreign conflicts pertaining to the Turkish state's painful transition. To that end, the state structure would have to assume the double task of reforming itself and transforming the conflicts hindering reform. Even if it might sound like a gargantuan undertaking, Turkey has done it before when the stars were aligned to bring together domestic concert and strong foreign support for reform. A peaceful transition in Turkey is not exclusively a Turkish issue; it would have broader geostrategic repercussions. Thus the Turkish state would have to reconsider its foreign policy alignments and, particularly, seek a more cooperative and consultative relationship with the European Union (EU).[6]

The question of why Turkish reform should be Western-oriented has a specific historical and cultural background. The fallacy that Turkey has a distinctive state tradition separate from the West overlooks the fact that the Turkish state is a product of Western modernization. What differentiates Turkey from its regional rivals; namely, Iran and, to a lesser extent, Russia, is its stronger adherence to Western thinking in terms of state organization. The Turkish quest to be part of the Western state system facilitated the growth of the Turkish democratic political system and has, to a certain extent, arrested authoritarian tendencies in the state-society relationship. This background has laid the groundwork for the development and consolidation of democratic demands and a democratic worldview, especially among urbanites and professionals, the backbone of Turkish society. Therefore, the Turkish identity crisis, partly stemming from the loss of direction in the West, especially with Brexit and the rise of Trumpist populism around the world, is unlikely, in the long run, to change Turkish society's alignment to better itself and its state institutions. Despite all ebbs and flows, Turkey has the necessary experience and expertise, and, most important, the will to reform its politics for further liberalization and extension of civil rights.[7]

This rethinking should start with the Turkish state's conflict resolution roles, transcending traditional approaches in favor of conciliatory formulas. The current course, particularly after July 15, has revitalized the security state but eroded the democratic state. As leaders in AKP circles have also conceded,[8] this erosion not only puts into doubt the sustainability of political stability, but also is likely to aggravate the state, security, and foreign policy crises. The presidential system is still a controversial issue. The government is seeking fixes to legitimize it, while the opposition vows to abandon it all together if elected. Here the core issue is less about the choice between managerialism and parliamentarianism, and more about the instrumentalization of the presidential system for personal choices, and maximum discretion and favor given to the security state. To move ahead, reform attempts need, first and foremost, to arrest the personality and security traits of the evolving systemic change.

Looking at the conflict resolution role of the state through Hendrix's prism, the strategy is to reject any power-sharing scheme with nonstate actors, despite the fact that such organizations may provide "dual benefits of creating complements between the diverse mechanisms, . . . as well as guarding against implementation failure in any particular dimension."[9] The main problem with this self-inflicted barrier to reform is that the whole process might run the risk of reaching a point to challenge stateness, which is a sanctuary of the state elite to justify their policies. The Weberian definition of the state as the entity that can claim a monopoly on the legitimate use of violence within a given territory[10] here stands in stark contrast to the state's responsibility for conflict resolution. The state is expected to use nonviolent methods to transform and desecuritize conflict situations. Mohammed Ayoob underlines the relationship between state building and conflict in the context of territorial consolidation and institution building.[11] State processes constitute the untouchable core of stateness in Turkey, and state elites have coercive power at their control to protect this sphere for themselves. The Turkish state has characteristics of not only a weak state, considering weak institutionalization and a low level of social cohesion, but also a strong state, which looks at managing capacity and coercive plus co-optative measures to deal with internal conflicts. What is deficient in the Turkish case is the understanding that peace is a coproduced process, and there is a need for more governance capacity in conflict resolution to minimize the need to employ coercive power.

To overcome this conflictual pattern, dating back to early state and nation building practices, Turkey's educational system needs to recognize peace education as a necessary way toward the healing process. Peace education should be taught not only within the public education system but also in institutional departments responsible for job training. However, state practices in education evade this domestic healing process and impose standards that make it difficult to use peace education to alleviate conflict in Turkey. Teachers and administrators have many difficulties with state authorities when they try to conduct peace education due to the suspicions attached to the subject.[12] They may face local and national pressures, as well as media exposure, as punishment for their efforts to promote peace education. As a former member of parliament with a background in Kurdish politics pointed out, "A seminar on nonviolent resistance may easily become an act to call for uprising and terrorist activity in Dersim. There is no culture of tolerance to any activity promoting peace in the security forces."[13]

As a reflection, the Turkish state's master narrative of the most important challenge to it, namely the Kurdish problem, is structured around terrorism, separation, foreign intervention, and economic backwardness. This mostly monolithic narrative categorically rebukes nuance and alternative historical accounts in counternarratives. According to Özden Melis Uluğ and J. Christopher Cohrs, "The rights, freedom, and democracy frame and the independence frame might be seen as different varieties of the Kurdish master narrative."[14] However, the state conflict resolution approach sees such differences or alternative thinking as separatist attempts to hide secret aims to divide the country and thus pose an existential threat to Turkey.[15]

There is a strong incentive within multiethnic states like Turkey to "fight against early separatists in order to deter additional separatists later on."[16] The state's forceful response to challengers signals an administrative trade-off to deter subsequent ethnic, societal, and other conflicts. A state's conflict resolution role is also a matter of reputation in a multidimensional sense. The first dimension is the ability to put the necessary capabilities together for effective mitigation or transformation of the conflict. Second is the issue of legitimacy, which means careful employment of justifiable and acceptable norms and means in the measures against the conflict. The Turkish state's conflict resolution is problematic in both of these dimensions. The choice of oppression over accommodation creates problems in conflict resolution processes. There is no serious attention to the issue of subsequent challengers and reputation in domestic and international public opinion.

Reforming Foreign and Security Policy

Turkey's foreign and security policy have resuscitated the bureaucratic-authoritarian tradition in Turkish foreign policy, albeit in a new form. In the new era the resuscitated traditional model of status quoism absent Western orientation automatically assigned the security cadres a prevalent role in policy making and implementation. In the post–July 15 era, partly due to the coalition dynamics with the MHP, the AKP government co-opted the military and intelligence apparatus in its quest for damage control amid the state crisis. Thus the security apparatus recovered its earlier role in foreign policy, and counterinsurgency methods trumped diplomacy and foreign policy coalition making. In this realist understanding of international relations, Turkish foreign policy acted more and more independent of alliance dynamics, particularly with regard to NATO and the EU.

Turkey's experience with the Syrian crisis and the revival of the PKK threat in a broader geography was a huge blow for pro-Atlanticist and pro-EU elements in Ankara. Not only did NATO fail to support Turkish security in Syria, particularly in the context of the rising threat of Russia, which culminated in the downing of the Russian jet in November 2015 and hit to another level during the Idlib crisis in March 2020, but also NATO and the EU failed to prop up Turkish democracy at its darkest hour; namely, July 15 and its aftermath, and even worse, they harbored Gülenists and putschists in European capitals. The US decision to cooperate with the PKK's Syrian offshoot and certain EU countries', above all France's and Germany's, public support for the PKK's role in Syria undermined the sense of alliance and commitment to the Western security community.

As a result, the Turkish state felt it had to assume a self-designed way to act to defend its national interests, at times contradicting the political and security identities of NATO and the EU. Thus Syria and Iraq again became realms of securitized foreign policy, and Turkey appeared ready to cooperate with Russia and Iran to make up for its failing Western security identity. The question of whether this disalignment was tactical or strategic is another issue; in any case, it does not change the fact that Turkey needs to introduce hybrid formulas to protect its core national interests.

However, one major problem has been the loss of communication channels: most important, trust and confidence between Turkey and its NATO allies, above all the United States and Germany. Again, this had to do, even if partly, with eroding institutional capacity and growing partisanship in Turkish foreign policy. The presidential system failed to make up for this deficit due to the lack of expertise and networks to disseminate targeted messages to avert unnecessary crises with the United States and European allies at a time of critical political transition.

Even worse, the post–July 15 atmosphere narrowed the chances of rethinking in foreign policy. At its hour of need, the government had to return to the security state to chart a conflictual course to fight back foreign and security crises. Rogue elements defending Russian, Chinese, and Iranian security ties were given leeway alongside the government's defamation of NATO and the Western alliance, which was accused of supporting, if not masterminding, the July 15 coup attempt. This was largely because civilian and academic input has been absent, and alternative thinking was considered tantamount to opposition to the defense of national interests. Even institutional feedback from the Ministry of Foreign Affairs remained minimal due both to the growing role of the presidency in foreign policy and the ministry's eroding human capacity after the purges.

To overcome this vicious circle of conflicts aggravated by eroding institutional capacity, and to cope with multiple challenges beyond the use of military-security tools, the need to refocus on building civilian institutional capacity has become more urgent. Certainly domestic consolidation is a governmental priority, and political transition would still trump all other concerns. Yet in any case a reinvigorated institutional setup, new thinking, and a multidisciplinary approach could pay off. Emphasis on diplomacy and better representation could open new venues for explaining and finding an audience for legitimate Turkish interests. The ability to voice diplomats' input, either through public diplomacy or behind closed doors, would motivate qualified public servants to engage more in policy making and implementation. Again, Turkey's return to international diplomacy as a responsible and respectable actor would better serve its interests both politically and economically.

The need for reform in Turkish foreign policy mainly stems from the loss of guiding principles in organization and policy formulation. Credibility entails upholding the principle of continuity in state affairs. Bureaucracy's ideally long-term vision is supposed to keep track of state records and pursue national interests. Their network with both national and international interlocutors shapes policy making and makes sure different stakes are taken into consideration. Yet the undeclared fight between the government and the bureaucracy has endangered this assumed long-term vision and diminished the bureaucracy's ability to steer an autonomous course as it acts under the government's ruling mandate. The dialectical dynamics of assigning the bureaucracy an all-in or submissive role has disrupted the state apparatus's ability to sustain the state memory, which has run the risk of alienating partners and emboldening adversaries.

Indisputably the agents of foreign and security policy making are in dire need of reform. The Ministry of Foreign Affairs lost its traditional role and failed to produce a working ethos to catch up with the political changes in Ankara and beyond. The military suffered large-scale purges and lost its interest in its traditional claim to become actively involved in policy making. Academia, and likewise civil society, is bleeding due to large-scale purges, infringements on academic independence, and the crowding out of independent thinking. The current style of overarching personal policy making without institutional feedback has not been able to fill this void. Moreover, following the uncertainties of constitutional transition and the resultant deficiency of a practical understanding of the government-bureaucracy relationship, the bureaucracy has automatically been excluded from the policy making process. Finally, the foreign and security institutions have had to struggle against burgeoning personnel and resource deficits, which also demoralized the bureaucracy and eroded its founding ethos as the servant of the nation.

Against these setbacks, a three-pronged set of measures should be put in place. The first priority should be to bring back meritocracy and revitalize the bureaucratic ethos to serve the nation. The formidable task of employing new bureaucratic cadres is therefore both a chance and a menace. If the political authority seizes this opportunity to seek efficiency and long-term commitment, Turkey still has qualified public officials as career professionals and a young and educated pool to employ to make up for the purges. Providing additional resources and fringe benefits, and above all, giving the bureaucracy a stake in policy making could be employed to better motivate the current cadres. If partisan considerations prevail, the state crisis will be prolonged, with damaging repercussions for state performance. Second, at a time of economic bottlenecks, more efficient use of available resources is obligatory. Prioritization rather than quantitative expansion in public service—such as the goal of maximizing the number of diplomatic missions across the globe—would serve Turkish interests better.

Third, the government should lose no time in reforming the legal framework for the relationship between political principles and the bureaucracy. The current uncertainty only breeds more uncertainty and leads to further stalling tactics on the part of the bureaucracy. The latter needs a road map, confidence, and applicable rules and procedures to implement and keep track of governmental policies. Finally, the purges and counterpurges have minimized trust and undermined esprit de corps, giving rise to revanchism and new cliques competing to eliminate rivals in bureaucracy. Therefore, political and objective supervision to make sure a bureaucratic ethos and meritocracy are restored needs to become a priority in prospective reform programs.

Government circles might think that inconsistency is an asset against uncontrollable instability both at home and abroad. It might also confuse the electorate to avert attention from burgeoning political and economic problems. It could even be thought to work in derailing a reasonable government-opposition debate, which again supposedly gives the government an upper hand with its control of media and messaging outlets in Turkey. These largely domestic goals, however, mar Turkey's interests and its ability to gain international support for foreign policy goals. Every day an internal debate in Turkey reaches an international audience, on either social media or specific national channels, it at best engenders mockery, and at worse plays into anti-Turkish feelings.[17] The overzealous claim to agitate the domestic electorate against assumed external deceit and animosity is further aggravated by the personalized use of social media to attract attention. When a tweet or retweet pops up in any corner of the world about Turkey or Turkish history, it immediately enters the national agenda, and the official response it gets from government circles turns into a bilateral or multilateral debate.[18] The progovernment media also plays a leading role in further alienating foreign partners.

In contemporary fashion, Turkey needs to act as a performing state and espouse the best practices of good governance. The former is about providing security and public goods, the latter is about transparency, accountability, and pluralism. Turkish policy makers cannot confine their immediate goals to providing the first and shelving the latter for sunnier days. As the dialectic clash of state and societal powers in recent history exemplifies, there is a proven, direct correlation between good governance and state power that is needed to strike a balance in the proper rule of the country. These principles are also valid for foreign and security policy making. Without state power, the rhetorical ability to perpetuate the ultimate Turkish goals of security and prosperity is nil. Without good governance, public support for and sustainability of policy and political agendas will prove merely temporary.

These goals are also a call for reinvigorating institutional setups and extending a greater share in foreign policy to stakeholders in civil society, academia, and relevant societal groups. Turkey cannot waive its earlier commitment to the societal-pluralist paradigm in foreign policy: Pandora's box has already been opened. As seen under the emergency rule and through the political leadership's securitization of survivalist concerns, Turkish society is ripe for participation in policy making and would welcome the reinstatement of its stakeholder position. This more than ever entails rebuilding state institutions with academic and societal feedback. Turkey needs expertise, division of labor, a multidisciplinary approach, and representation of multiculturalism in foreign policy. The differentiation of sources of policy making would broaden public support and would also put up a barrier against taking narrow-minded and one-sided approaches in foreign and security policy in Turkey. Bearing in mind Turkey's pluralistic turn would ease the elitist course to set an exclusive foreign policy for Turkey and broaden the foreign policy vision, which is currently based on narrow security priorities. On the other hand, a blend of academic, societal, and pluralistic input would enrich Turkish foreign policy and bring in the much-needed organic link with Turkey's neighborhood. Only if Turkish foreign and security institutions make the most of this pluralism can Turkey play up to its role as a muscular regional power.

Conclusion

Provided the reform process finds the right course to entrench the basics of the new system, the government would have a better chance of introducing a change in the bureaucratic culture. Even that, however, would entail good working relations between the government and the bureaucracy in order to pursue these broader goals. High-level bureaucrats may not turn easily into managers of the new system, and outside appointments may not easily fill the required positions. There needs to be careful work toward picking ideal candidates as new civil servants are hired and promoted from among the bureaucracy and nonpublic officials. Bureaucrats need future job security and career opportunities to adapt to their new roles in the assumed transition. Despite the growth of the private sector in Turkey, the public sector still has qualified and highly educated cadres, particularly in career-based institutions. Given the current gap in human resources and unpreparedness for a decisive turn, cohabitation between the political and bureaucratic cadres is the most feasible option at every stage.

Earlier attempts for state reform simply avoided engagement in public debate. Consultation with the public on the ways and means of civil service that they would like to receive would enrich the reform process as this would provide feedback from a vital stakeholder. The involvement of civil society, interest groups, and societal actors in this process would democratize and legitimize the process. Overall, state reform is not a one-off decision. A multiphased approach that would expand the pros of reform, ideally in regard to good governance, appears to be a reasonable recipe. In any case, the reform process has to take into account the current realities in Turkey. The education of the prospective cadres should go hand in hand with the learning process of the bureaucrats presently in charge. The quest for uniformity will certainly breed large-scale resistance from different sectors of the state and society. Thus the ultimate goal in state reform should be a consensual and pluralist transition in order to minimize this backlash and to elevate the quality of public service in Turkey.

Conclusion

Reform or Conflict?

The Turkey of early 2021 is far from the image of an associate of reform, reconciliation, and rising soft power in global politics that it was at the turn of the millennium. Certainly, this disparaged image is not merely Turkey's making. The rise of populism and authoritarianism on the global stage did not create a favorable environment for consensual politics and expansion of democratic regimes. Turkey is a country surrounded by burgeoning geostrategic crises in all directions. The rise of Russia and Putinism, compounded and also assisted by the incessant Syrian civil war, jihadism, and the empowerment of anti-Westernism and multipolarity in Turkey's neighborhood, contributed to Turkey's sliding democratic credentials. Even worse, Brexit and migrant crises undid Turkey's vision for inclusion in the European Union (EU), as well as the EU's own enlargement project of democratic and pluralist transition in the broader neighborhood. While the EU turned inward and, disputably, against its core values, Turkey's ability to sustain the democratization process proved infeasible. The US rebuke of its own leadership role during the latter term of the Obama administration, and its twisted and mostly transgressive form during Trump's presidency has undermined the Turkish ability to stand alone in a region of instability and rising chaos as a pro-Western actor. It is only a matter of time before we see whether the tension between the newly elected Biden administration in the US and Turkish government will result in a change in the Turkish role in regional politics and on the international scene.

Yet Turkey's crises are mostly self-inflicted and could have been ameliorated with proper state leadership. Turkey's current state, political, security, and foreign policy crises were more the result of mismanagement and political infighting than a predetermined result of structural conflicts. Its long-ignored state-society relationship was a major factor in overturning the Turkish case for reform and conflict resolution. The Turkish state's binary conflict resolution approach fell short of resolving complex political and social conflicts in Turkey. Therefore, the need for change in the state's conflict resolution role is paramount and, in many ways, existential. The Turkish polity needs to resolve many of its present dilemmas in order to sustain the provision of basic public goods, such as security and stability. It would be wise for policy makers to work toward democratic consolidation and the rule of law to set the stage for a more comprehensive political and cultural shift in state-led conflict resolution efforts in Turkey. To that end, Turkish policy makers need to bear in mind that the political crisis gave rise to polarization and deinstitutionalization, which have resulted in deadly blows to administrative power and have served as strong barriers to good governance. The state crisis intensifies the urgent call for reform, but political polarization and deinstitutionalization make it nearly impossible for the willing parties to pursue a reform agenda. The post–July 15 atmosphere has crowded out the case for reconciliatory reform, and the state apparatus in the leadership of political cadres has put a disproportionate focus on security. The perceived success in securing the streets and warding off terror threats, which reached an unbearable level in late 2015, overshadowed the need to secure minds and hearts. The ongoing mood of emergency law undermined social trust, professionalism, entrepreneurship, and a broader perception of justice. In the ensuing Manichaean climate, the Justice and Development Party (AKP) government—and more broadly the supporters of the People's Alliance (Cumhur İttifakı, which comprises the AKP and the Nationalist Action Party, or MHP)—were directly pitted against the National Alliance (Millet İttifakı, which includes the Republican People's Party, or CHP, and the Good Party, or IP, and its supporters, the People's Democratic Party, or HDP, and the Felicity Party, or SP).[1]

Against the gloomy backdrop of unprecedented state crisis aggravated by growing political polarization, Turkey has been facing a major challenge in setting the contours of the new presidential system. The emergence of the presidential system has failed to affirm the basis of a peaceful and conciliatory transition, which ended in a coup attempt and the state of emergency in its aftermath. This scenario was nearly unimaginable for many Turkey analysts just a few years ago. The systemic change has instead been a corollary of the government versus military, government versus Fethullah Gülen, AKP versus all, and AKP versus AKP rifts, which minimized the ability to sketch a broader and more feasible system of government. The ongoing regime change has yet to produce a new constitution that would define the roles and prerogatives of the constitutional organs with a broader vision of government and society. In this constructed world of ambiguities, it is everyone's guess as to the direction of Turkey and the Turkish polity.

The immediate effects of this haphazard transition effectively undermined, and at times expunged, the workings of the state apparatus. Without a clearly defined division of labor between the government and the bureaucracy, there emerged nothing but confusion, stagnation, and ultimate gray zones, as well as a state ruled by arbitrariness and singular interests. Overreliance on the president and his office has been a major risk, which was largely ignored by partisan considerations. The presumed goal of neutralizing bureaucratic tutelage was separated from the means to realize the assumed goal of managerialism and efficiency. Following the coup attempt, emergency rule was instrumentalized to defy the emergence of alternative thinking, and was devoid of a clear division of labor and delegation of authority. The tendency to centralize all decision making rendered any attempt to address the complex crises even more infeasible. Quick fixes, such as the establishment of presidential committees and newly constituted councils, were far from an adequate substitute for the policy making role of the former constitutional order. Political appointments were mostly nepotistic and controversial. Even the technocratic Council of Ministers fell short of expectations for unimpeded performance.[2]

The state and political crises also created obstacles for the long-awaited reset in Turkish foreign and security policy. Despite all expectations for fence-mending, Turkey has been unable to minimize its conflict map and maximize its zones of cooperation. The end result of Turkey's failure to introduce a more conciliatory discourse on foreign policy has been that Turkish foreign policy is today more and more defined by hard power in regional policy, Eurasianist policy premises, accord and even bandwagoning with a revisionist Russia, and failure to repair deteriorating Western ties with the United States and the EU. President Recep Tayyip Erdoğan's overarching personal role has sidelined the traditional levers of policy making and failed to build the necessary institutional capacity to fill the void. The end result has been consolidated personal and partisan prerogatives in foreign policy, narrowed room for maneuver in regional and international policy, and inconsistent policy agendas imposed on the bureaucracy.

The foreign and security crises not only further locked Turkey into a series of international conflicts, such as the Syria conflict and growing divergences with the United States, but also undermined the case for reform in Turkey. The latter was a function of the first, as the insecurity-breeds-insecurity syndrome: the inability to stabilize the political order in Turkey hindered a possible course to implement or even ponder a feasible way for reform. Without a major mechanism to pull Turkey toward reform, Turkish leadership fell short on its earlier commitment to further liberalization and democratization. With the United States and the EU turning more and more exclusive and insular due to domestic challenges, Turkey proved unable to set the course on its own. On the contrary, intensified geostrategic rivalries, which brought Russia into the scene as a major player in Turkish foreign policy, have impeded the development of a consensual reform agenda in Turkey and aggravated the domestic cleavages on Westernism, the role of Islam in politics, and the Kurdish question.

A consensual approach to governing in the aftermath of the failed coup could have minimized the impact of political and systemic crises in the state apparatus and in foreign and security policy. Instead, polarization has come to rule the day. Given that neither the systemic and political crises at home nor the security and geostrategic crises abroad are likely to disappear soon, there is a need to rise above short-termism and to introduce institution building and capacity building in the state apparatus—and, reflexively, in foreign and security policy. The most pressing issues reflected in these crises are generating capacity, institution building, and interagency coordination among traditional and new agencies. If the half-hearted and short-term measures accompanied by partisan attitudes under the duress of political and systemic crises are to prevail in the long term, this would lead to broader failures in state administration and would further aggravate the crisis mode in foreign policy.

Against this background, it is urgent to first and foremost rethink bureaucratic reform. First, policy makers need to bear in mind that high-level bureaucrats may not turn easily into managers of the new system, and outside appointments may not easily fill the required positions. There needs to be careful work toward picking ideal candidates as new civil servants, who would be hired and promoted from among the bureaucracy and nonpublic officials. Second, given the current gap in human resources and the unpreparedness for a decisive turn, cohabitation between the political and bureaucratic cadres is the most feasible option at every stage. Third, earlier attempts at state reform simply avoided engagement in public debate. Consultation with the public on the ways and means of government services would reinforce the reform process, as this would provide feedback from a vital stakeholder. Fourth, education of the prospective cadres should go hand in hand with continuing education and training of the bureaucrats presently in charge. All these measures work toward a clear constitutional definition of the emerging polity.

In fragmented, multicultural, and multiconfessional societies, finding the right tone within a grand narrative has always proved a challenging task. A decade ago Turkey came close to finding one, but it backtracked due to a series of impediments, and then turned against this ideal. The current crisis should provide incentives to turn the tide and get back on track toward a reformist course. Despite the hardships of recent years, Turkish society has demonstrated its desire for normalcy. Turkey's democratic credentials were eroded but still on display recently in the rerun of the mayoral elections in İstanbul in June 2019. Therefore, the state elites need to respond to this desire for normalcy and consensual administration. Revitalizing a multiphased approach that would expand the pros of reform and integrate factional, regional, confessional, and sectoral grievances into the reform agenda, ideally on the basis of the broader goal of good governance, appears to be a good recipe for reform. The ultimate reform model should entail a consensual and pluralist transition in order to minimize backlash and elevate the quality of public services required to implement the much-needed Turkish reform.

Notes

Bibliography

Index

Notes

1. Turkey's Political Crisis

1. Lucio Biasiori and Giuseppe Marcocci, *Machiavelli, Islam, and the East: Reorienting the Foundations of Modern Political Thought* (Cham, Switzerland: Palgrave Macmillan, 2018).

2. Şerif Mardin, "Center-Periphery Relations: A Key to Turkish Politics?," *Daedalus* 102, no. 1 (1973): 169–90, www.jstor.org/stable/20024114.

3. Turkey was officially declared a candidate country for EU membership in the EU Helsinki Summit in December 1999.

4. Zafer Yılmaz, "The AKP and the Spirit of the 'New' Turkey: Imagined Victim, Reactionary Mood, and Resentful Sovereign," *Turkish Studies* 18, no. 3 (2017): 482–513, doi.org/10.1080/14683849.2017.1314763.

5. Duygu Ersoy and Fahriye Üstüner, "'Liberal Intellectuals' Narration of the Justice and Development Party in Turkey," *Turkish Studies* 17, no. 3 (2016): 406–28, doi.org/10.1080/14683849.2016.1166057.

6. Metin Heper, "The Strong State as a Problem for the Consolidation of Democracy: Turkey and Germany Compared," *Comparative Political Studies* 25, no. 2 (1992): 176, doi.org/10.1177/0010414092025002002.

7. Neşe Düzel, "Interview with Baskın Oran," *Radikal* (İstanbul), June 4, 2007, http://acikradyo.com.tr/arsiv-icerigi/baskin-oranla-soylesi.

8. Vali Nasr, *The Rise of Islamic Capitalism: Why the New Muslim Middle Class Is the Key to Defeating Extremism* (New York: Free Press, 2010).

9. See, Meliha Benli Altunışık, "The Turkish Model and Democratization in the Middle East," *Arab Studies Quarterly* 27, nos. 1/2 (2005): 45–63, www.jstor.org/stable/41859009.

10. Ali Kemal Özcan, *Turkey's Kurds in Perspective: A Theoretical Analysis of Abdullah Öcalan and the PKK* (London: Routledge, 2006).

11. M. Hakan Yavuz and Nihat Ali Özcan, "Turkish Democracy and the Kurdish Question," *Middle East Policy* 24, no. 4 (2015): 73–87, doi.org/10.1111/mepo.12159.

12. "Erdoğan'ın Diyarbakır Mesajı: Devlet Geçmişte Hatalar Yaptı," *Radikal* (İstanbul), August 13, 2005, www.radikal.com.tr/politika/erdoganin-diyarbakir-mesaji-devlet-gecmiste-hatalar-yapti-754621/.

13. Hadi Uluengin, "Arınç'ın Manifestosu," *Hürriyet* (İstanbul), April 25, 2006, www.hurriyet.com.tr/arinc-in-manifestosu-4309821.

14. Ümit Cizre, "Demythologyzing the National Security Concept: The Case of Turkey," *Middle East Journal* 57, no. 2 (2003): 213–29.

15. Cevat Öneş, "Güvenlik ve Demokrasi," *Radikal* (İstanbul), December 28, 2005.

16. Bülent Aras and Rabia Karakaya Polat, "From Conflict to Cooperation: Desecuritization of Turkey's Relations with Syria and Iran," *Security Dialogue* 39, no. 5 (2008): 475–95, doi.org/10.1177/0967010608096150.

17. Aras and Polat, "From Conflict.".

18. Ferhat Kentel and Gevorg Poghosyan, *Ermenistan ve Türkiye Vatandaşları Karşılıklı Algılama ve Diyalog Projesi* (İstanbul: TESEV, 2005).

19. TÜSIAD, *Türk Demokrasisi'nde 130 Yıl (1876–2006): Prof. Bülent Tanör'ün Anısına Türkiye'de Demokratikleşme Perspektifleri 10. Yıl Güncellemesi*, report no. TÜSIAD-T/2006-12/426 (İstanbul: TÜSIAD, 2006), https://tusiad.org/tr/yayinlar/raporlar/item/5290-turk-demokrasisinde-130-yil-1876-2006.

20. Hakkı Taş, "A History of Turkey's AKP-Gülen Conflict," *Mediterranean Politics* 23, no. 3 (2018): 397, doi.org/10.1080/13629395.2017.1328766.

21. "Büyükanıt'ın Konuşmasının Tam Metni," *Hürriyet* (İstanbul), April 12, 2006, www.hurriyet.com.tr/gundem/buyukanitin-konusmasinin-tam-metni-6321761.

22. "'AK Parti Kapatılmasın' Kararı Çıktı," *Milliyet* (İstanbul), July 30, 2008, www.milliyet.com.tr/siyaset/ak-parti-kapatilmasin-karari-cikti-972729.

23. The president of the Supreme Court, declaring the decision of the Court, underlined the need to deescalate polarization in Turkish society and called on all political parties to seek common ground for constitutional reform to avoid a repetition of such court cases. See "'AK Parti Kapatılmasın.'"

24. Ergun Özbudun, "Turkey's Judiciary and the Drift toward Competitive Authoritarianism," *The International Spectator* 50, no. 2 (2015): 42–45, doi.org/10.1080/03932729.2015.1020651.

25. Taş, "History," 397.

26. Interview with a former member of parliament, Ankara, November 23, 2017.

27. Markus V. Hoehne, "Limits of Hybrid Political Orders: The Case of Somaliland," *Journal of Eastern African Studies* 7, no. 2 (2013): 200, doi.org/10.1080/17531055.2013.776279.

28. Nicole Pope, "Turkey: Marching toward One-Man Rule," *Journal of International Affairs* 71, no. 1 (2017): 17–30, www.jstor.org/stable/26494361.

29. M. Hakan Yavuz, "Understanding Turkish Secularism in the 21th Century: A Contextual Roadmap," *Southeast European and Black Sea Studies* 19, no. 1 (2019): 55–78, doi.org/10.1080/14683857.2019.1576367.

30. Jenny White, "Spindle Autocracy in the New Turkey," *Brown Journal of World Affairs* 24, no. 1 (2017), http://bjwa.brown.edu/24-1/spindle-autocracy-in-the-new-turkey/.

31. Fatih Ceran, "From Paradigm Shift to Retooling: The Foundation and Maintenance of the AKP," *Southeast European and Black Sea Studies* 19, no. 1 (2019): 175–93, doi.org/10.1080/14683857.2019.1579858.

32. Berk Esen and Şebnem Gümüşçü, "Rising Competitive Authoritarianism in Turkey," *Third World Quarterly* 37, no. 9 (2016): 1583, doi.org/10.1080/01436597.2015.1135732. See also Bahar Başer and Ahmet Erdi Öztürk, *Authoritarian Politics in Turkey: Elections, Resistance, and the AKP* (London: Bloomsbury, 2017).

33. Ersin Kalaycıoğlu, "The Conundrum of Coalition Politics in Turkey," *Turkish Studies* 17, no. 1 (2016): 31, doi.org/10.1080/14683849.2015.1136087.

34. Orçun Selçuk, "Strong Presidents and Weak Institutions: Populism in Turkey, Venezuela, and Ecuador," *Southeast European and Black Sea Studies* 16, no. 4 (2016): 583.

35. Selçuk, "Strong Presidents," 571.

36. Michael M. Gunter, "Erdogan and the Decline of Turkey," *Middle East Policy* 23, no. 4 (2016): 123–35, doi.org/10.1111/mepo.12238.

37. Karabekir Akkoyunlu and Kerem Öktem, "Existential Insecurity and the Making of a Weak Authoritarian Regime in Turkey," *Southeast European and Black Sea Studies* 16, no. 4 (2016): 505–27, doi.org/10.1080/14683857.2016.1253225.

38. Necati Polat, *Regime Change in Contemporary Turkey: Politics, Rights, Mimesis* (Edinburgh, Scotland: Edinburgh Univ. Press, 2016), 6.

39. Polat, *Regime Change*, 11.

40. Akkoyunlu and Öktem, "Existential Insecurity."

41. Polat, *Regime Change*, 6.

42. Akkoyunlu and Öktem, "Existential Insecurity."

43. Selçuk, "Strong Presidents."

44. Emre Turkut, "Accommodating Security Imperatives v. Protecting Fundamental Rights: The Challenge of States of Emergency in the Context of Countering Terrorism in Turkey," *Security and Human Rights* 28 (2019): 62–91, doi.org/10.1163/18750230-02801002.

45. "Kurdish Solution Process Will Continue: Turkish PM," *Anadolu Agency*, March 14, 2014, www.aa.com.tr/en/turkey/kurdish-solution-process-will-continue-turkish-pm/174736.

46. "Abdullah Öcalan'ın 2014 Newroz Mesajı," *Yüksekova Haber* (Hakkari), March 21, 2014, www.yuksekovahaber.com.tr/haber/abdullah-ocalanin-2014-newroz-mesaji-125867.htm. http://www.yuksekovahaber.com/haber/abdullah-ocalanin-2014-newroz-mesaji-125867.htm.

47. Muharrem Yılmaz, "'Çözüme Yatırım' ve Bölgesel Kalkınma," *TÜSİAD Görüş Dergisi* (2013): 13–18, https://tusiad.org/tr/tum/item/6861-tusiad-yonetim-kurulu-baskani-muharrem-yilmazin-gorus-dergisinin-temmuz-2013-sayisinda-yayinlanan-cozume-yatirim-ve-bolgesel-kalkinma-baslikli-makalesi.

48. "Terörün Toplam Maliyetini Açıkladı," *Milliyet* (İstanbul), October 26, 2013, www.milliyet.com.tr/ekonomi/terorun-toplam-maliyetini-acikladi-1782715.

49. Burak Bilgehan Özpek, "The State's Changing Role regarding the Kurdish Question of Turkey: From Consistent Tutelage to Volatile Securitization," *Alternatives: Global, Local, Political* 44, no. 1 (2019): 38, doi.org/10.1177/0304375419854599.

50. "Erdoğan: 400 Milletvekili Lazım," *Milliyet* (İstanbul), February 6, 2015, www.milliyet.com.tr/siyaset/erdogan-400-milletvekili-lazim-2009741.

51. Ahmet Erdi Öztürk, "An Alternative Reading of Religion and Authoritarianism: The New Logic between Religion and State in the AKP's New Turkey," *Southeast European and Black Sea Studies* 19, no. 1 (2019): 79–98, doi.org/10.1080/14683857.2019.1576370.

52. Syaza Farhana Mohamad Shukri and Ishtiaq Hossain, "Strategic Shifts in Discourse by the AKP in Turkey, 2002–2015," *Mediterranean Quarterly* 28, no. 3 (2017): 5–26, doi.org/10.1215/10474552-4216388.

53. "Fethullah Gülen: İsrail'den İzin Almaliydilar," *NTV* (İstanbul), April 6, 2010, www.ntv.com.tr/dunya/fethullah-gulen-israilden-izin-almaliydilar,kIC_HTknIEavwlzh-VOxdg.

54. Yavuz, "Understanding Turkish Secularism."

55. Öztürk, "Alternative Reading," 94.

56. Samuel P. Huntington, *The Third Wave: Democratization in the Late Twentieth Century* (Norman: Univ. of Oklahoma Press, 1991).

57. Paul Brooker, *Non-Democratic Regimes* (Basingstoke, UK: Palgrave Macmillan, 2014).

58. Larry Diamond, "Facing Up to the Democratic Recession," *Journal of Democracy* 26, no. 1 (2015): 144, doi.org/10.1353/jod.2015.0009.

59. Steven Heydemann and Reinoud Leenders, "Authoritarian Learning and Authoritarian Resilience: Regime Responses to the 'Arab Awakening,'" *Globalizations* 8, no. 5 (2011): 647–53, doi.org/10.1080/14747731.2011.621274.

2. State and Institutions in Turkey

1. Johannes Lindvall and Jan Teorell, "State Capacity as Power: A Conceptual Framework," *STANCE Working Paper Series* 1 (2016): 1–18, https://portal.research.lu.se/portal/en/publications/state-capacity-as-power-a-conceptual-framework(ca52e85b-f17e-401d-9414-c5f52ec860e9).html#Overview. See also Johannes Lindvall, *Reform Capacity* (Oxford, UK: Oxford Univ. Press, 2017).

2. Carter V. Findley, *Bureaucratic Reform in the Ottoman Empire: The Sublime Porte, 1789–1922* (Princeton, NJ: Princeton Univ. Press, 1980).

3. Metin Heper, *The State Tradition in Turkey* (Beverley, UK: Eothen, 1985).

4. See Metin Heper and E. Fuat Keyman, "Double-Faced State: Political Patronage and the Consolidation of Democracy in Turkey," *Middle Eastern Studies* 34, no. 4 (1998): 259–77, doi.org/10.1080/00263209808701251.

5. Osman Turan, "The Ideal of World Domination among the Medieval Turks," *Studia Islamica*, no. 4 (1955): 77–90, doi.org/10.2307/1595052.

6. Halil İnalcık, *Osmanlı'da Devlet, Hukuk ve Adâlet* (İstanbul: Kronik), 2016.

7. See Metin Heper, "The Strong State as a Problem for the Consolidation of Democracy: Turkey and Germany Compared," *Comparative Political Studies* 25, no. 2 (1992): 169–94, doi.org/10.1177/0010414092025002002.

8. For a similar discussion, see Dan Slater and Sofia Fenner, "State Power and Staying Power: Infrastructural Mechanisms and Authoritarian Durability," *Journal of International Affairs* 65, no. 1 (2011): 15–29, www.jstor.org/stable/24388179.

9. Ömer Dinçer, *Türkiye'de Değişim Yapmak Neden Bu Kadar Zor?* (İstanbul: Alfa Basım Yayım, 2016).

10. Süleyman Sözen, "New Public Administration in Turkey," in *Turkey's Democratization Process*, ed. Carmen Rodríguez et al. (London: Routledge, 2014), 238.

11. Carol Migdalovitz, *Turkey's 2007 Elections: Crisis of Identity and Power* (Washington, DC: Congressional Research Service, 2007).

12. Barçın Yinanç, "Gülenists 'Abused' Efforts to Enhance Democracy: Ruling AKP Official," *Hurriyet Daily News* (İstanbul), July 17, 2017, www.hurriyetdailynews.com/gulenists-abused-efforts-to-enhance-democracy-ruling-akp-official-115570.

13. Barçın Yinanç, "Ample Evidence to Prove that Gülenists Were behind Turkey's Coup Attempt: Journalist Sedat Ergin," *Hurriyet Daily News* (İstanbul), August 28, 2017, www.hurriyetdailynews.com/ample-evidence-to-prove-that-gulenists-were-behind-turkeys-coup-attempt-journalist-sedat-ergin-117241.

14. Çiğdem Alyanak, "Erdoğan'dan Eğitim Ve Kültür Özeleştirisi," *Anadolu Ajansı*, February 9, 2017, www.memurlar.net/haber/645272/.

15. Interview with a member of parliament, Ankara, December 21, 2016.

16. Interview with a bureaucrat, Ankara, December 21, 2016.

17. Interview with a bureaucrat, Ankara, November 21, 2017.

18. James Masters and Becky Anderson, "Erdogan Insists Turkey Reforms Don't Make Him a Dictator," *CNN International*, April 18, 2017, www.cnn.com/2017/04/18/europe/erdogan-turkey-interview/index.html.

19. Andrew P. Cortell and Susan Peterson, "Limiting the Unintended Consequences of Institutional Change," *Comparative Political Studies* 34, no. 7 (2001): 793, doi.org/10.1177/0010414001034007003.

20. "Erdoğan's Declaration of 'System Change' Outrages Turkey's Opposition," *Hürriyet Daily News* (İstanbul), August 16, 2015, www.hurriyetdailynews.com/erdogans-declaration-of-system-change-outrages-turkeys-opposition--87036.

21. Bruce E. Moon and William J. Dixon, "Politics, the State, and Basic Human Needs: A Cross-National Study," *American Journal of Political Science* 29, no. 4 (1985): 661–94, www.jstor.org/stable/2111176.

22. Interview with a bureaucrat, Ankara, December 21, 2016.

23. David Andersen et al., "State Capacity and Political Regime Stability," *Democratization* 21, no. 7 (2014): 1305, doi.org/10.1080/13510347.2014.960204.

24. Michael Mann, "The Autonomous Power of the State: Its Origins, Mechanisms, and Results," *European Journal of Sociology / Archives Européennes De Sociologie* 25, no. 2 (1984): 188, doi.org/10.1017/S0003975600004239.

25. Mann, "Autonomous Power."

26. Orçun Selçuk, "Strong Presidents and Weak Institutions: Populism in Turkey, Venezuela, and Ecuador," *Southeast European and Black Sea Studies* 16, no. 4 (2016): 571–89, doi.org/10.1080/14683857.2016.1242893.

27. Interview with a member of parliament, Ankara, December 21, 2016.

28. Interview with a member of parliament, Ankara, December 21, 2016.

29. "AKP'nin Kamuda 'Uyum' Fırsatçılığı," *Cumhuriyet* (İstanbul), October 28, 2017, www.cumhuriyet.com.tr/haber/siyaset/854426/AKP_nin_kamuda__uyum__firsatciligi.htm.

30. Gökhan Gökçe, "Interview with Özlem Zengin," *TRT Haber* (İstanbul), February 15, 2017, www.youtube.com/watch?v=yGSqpQy7T4o.

31. Eva Etzioni-Halevy, *Bureaucracy and Democracy: A Political Dilemma* (London: Routledge & Kegan, 1985).

32. Hazal Ateş, "Memurluk Tapulu Mal Değil," *Sabah* (İstanbul), February 21, 2017, www.sabah.com.tr/ekonomi/2017/02/21/memurluk-tapulu-mal-degil.

33. James Q. Wilson, *Bureaucracy: What Government Agencies Do and Why They Do It* (New York: Basic Books, 2001).

34. Judith Tendler, *Good Government in the Tropics* (Baltimore, MD: Johns Hopkins Univ. Press, 1998); Akshay Mangla, "Bureaucratic Norms and State Capacity in India: Implementing Primary Education in the Himalayan Region," *Asian Survey* 55, no. 5 (2015): 882–908, doi.org/10.1525/as.2015.55.5.882.

35. Soner Çağaptay, *The New Sultan: Erdoğan and the Crisis of Modern Turkey* (London: I. B. Tauris, 2017).

36. "Turkey Locks Up Dissidents," *Economist*, November 10, 2016, www.economist.com/europe/2016/11/10/turkey-locks-up-dissidents.

37. Tacettin Karaer, "12 Eylül ve Türk Kamu Yönetiminin Yeniden Düzenlenmesi," *Amme İdaresi Dergisi* 20, no. 3 (1987): 29–54.

38. "Doğu Perinçek'ten Kritik Analiz 'Yargının Altın Devri,'" *Aydınlık* (İstanbul), June 6, 2017, www.aydinlik.com.tr/turkiye/2017-haziran/dogu-perincek-ten-kritik-analiz-yarginin-altin-devri.

39. Mustafa Mert Bildircin, "FETÖ'den Boşalan Yerler Yeni Tarikatlarla Dolduruldu," *BirGün* (İstanbul), August 11, 2017, www.birgun.net/haber-detay/fetoden-bosalan-yerler-yeni-tarikatlarla-dolduruldu-174268.html.

40. This is a main theme in progovernment circles, which justify the consolidation of power for the purpose of averting "looming" interventions against the government. See, Abdurrahman Dilipak, "Roller Netleşirken," *Yeni Akit* (İstanbul), November 4, 2017, http://m.yeniakit.com.tr/yazarlar/abdurrahman-dilipak/roller-netlesirken-21700.html.

41. Kemal Kılıçdaroğlu, "Tek Adam Değil, Parlamenter Sistem İstiyoruz," *CNN TÜRK* (İstanbul), July 9, 2017, www.cnnturk.com/video/turkiye/kilicdaroglu-tek-adam-degil-parlamenter-sistem-istiyoruz.

42. Gizem Karakış, "Yeni Sistemde Revizyon Çalışmaları Başladı," *Hürriyet* (İstanbul), July 13, 2019, www.hurriyet.com.tr/gundem/yeni-sistemde-revizyon-calismalari-basladi-41272592.

3. The Role of State in Conflict Resolution in Turkey

1. Metin Heper, "The Ottoman Legacy and Turkish Politics," *Journal of International Affairs* 54, no. 1 (Fall 2000): 66, www.jstor.org/stable/24357689.

2. Halil İnalcık, *Osmanlı'da Devlet, Hukuk ve Adâlet* (İstanbul: Kronik, 2016).

3. Heper, "Ottoman Legacy."

4. Musa Çadırcı, "Tanzimat'tan Cumhuriyet'e Ülke Yönetimi," in *Tanzimat'tan Cumhuriyet'e Türkiye Ansiklopedisi*, vol. 1, ed. Murat Belge (İstanbul: İletişim Yayınları, 1985), 230.

5. Şerif Mardin, "Center-Periphery Relations: A Key to Turkish Politics?" *Daedalus* 102, no. 1 (1973): 169–90, www.jstor.org/stable/i20024104.

6. Mardin, "Center-Periphery Relations," 186.

7. Kalevi J. Holsti, *The State, War, and the State of War* (Cambridge: Cambridge Univ. Press, 2004).

8. Interview with a journalist, İstanbul, October 17, 2017.

9. Interview with a local politician, Diyarbakır, October 22, 2018.

10. Interview with Sırrı Süreyya Önder, member of parliament from the People's Democratic Party (HDP), Ankara, November 21, 2017.

11. Mesut Yeğen, "The Kurdish Peace Process in Turkey: Genesis, Evolution, and Prospects," Global Turkey in Europe Working Paper no. 11 (2015): 3, www.iai.it/sites/default/files/gte_wp_11.pdf.

12. Rachel Suissa, "Conflict as a Learning Process: States Conflict versus State and Non-State Actor Conflict," *Defence Studies* 11, no. 2 (2011), doi.org/10.1080/14702436.2011.590395.

13. Önder interview.

14. Francis Fukuyama, *State-Building: Governance and World Order in the 21st Century* (Ithaca, NY: Cornell Univ. Press, 2004).

15. Interview with Fikri Sağlar, member of parliament from the CHP, Ankara, November 21, 2017.

16. Interview with Talip Küçükcan, member of parliament from the AKP, Ankara, November 21, 2017.

17. Sarah Elwood, "Beyond Cooptation or Resistance: Urban Spatial Politics, Community Organizations, and GIS-Based Spatial Narratives," *Annals of the Association of American Geographers* 96, no. 2 (2006): 323–41, doi.org/10.1111/j.1467-8306.2006.00480.x.

18. Erdem Yörük, "The Long Summer of Turkey: The Gezi Uprising and Its Historical Roots," *South Atlantic Quarterly* 113, no. 2, (2014): 419–26, doi.org/10.1215/00382876-2644203.

19. "Turk Halkina Atılan Tekme," *Deutsche Welle* (Ankara), May 16, 2014, https://www.dw.com/tr/türk-halkına-atılan-tekme/a-17640185.

20. Interview with a bureaucrat from prime ministry, Ankara, November 23, 2017.

21. Sağlar interview.

22. Yeğen, "The Kurdish Peace Process in Turkey."

23. Ersel Aydınlı and Nihat Ali Özcan, "The Conflict Resolution and Counterterrorism Dilemma: Turkey Faces Its Kurdish Question," *Terrorism and Political Violence* 23, no. 3 (2011): 438–57, doi.org/10.1080/09546553.2011.557328; Şaban Kardaş, "The Domestic-Regional Nexus in Turkey's Counterterrorism," *GMF on Turkey*, January 8, 2019, www.gmfus.org/publications/domestic-regional-nexus-turkeys-counterterrorism-policy.

24. For more information, see the Kamu Düzeni ve Güvenliği Müsteşarlığı (Undersecretariat of Public Order and Security) website: www.kdgm.gov.tr/?ax=kdgmalangsmainpage&l=en.

25. For the full text of the report, see "Toplumsal Barış Yollarının Araştırılması ve Çözüm Sürecinin Değerlendirilmesi Amaciyla Kurulan Meclis Araştırma Komisyonu Raporu" (Report of Parliament's Steering Committee for Inquiry of the Societal Peace and Resolution Process), http://tbmm.gov.tr/komisyon/cozum_sureci/docs/cozum_kom_raporu.pdf.

26. Interview with Haldun Solmaztürk, director of 21st Century Turkey Institute, Ankara, November 23, 2017.

4. The Crisis in Turkey's Foreign and Security Policy

1. Colin Hay, "Narrating Crisis: The Discursive Construction of the 'Winter of Discontent,'" *Sociology* 30, no. 2 (1996): 266, doi.org/10.1177/0038038596030002004.

2. Wesley W. Widmaier, Mark Blyth, and Leonard Seabrooke, "Exogenous Shocks or Endogenous Constructions?: The Meanings of Wars and Crises," *International Studies Quarterly* 51, no. 4 (2007): 748, doi.org/10.1111/j.1468-2478.2007.00474.x.

3. Charles F. Hermann, "Changing Course: When Governments Choose to Redirect Foreign Policy," *International Studies Quarterly* 34, no. 1 (1990): 5, doi.org/10.23 07/2600403.

4. Michael Barnett, "Culture, Strategy, and Foreign Policy Change: Israel's Road to Oslo," *European Journal of International Relations* 5, no. 1 (1999): 8–9, doi.org/10.1177/1 354066199005001001.

5. Ali L. Karaosmanoğlu, "The Evolution of the National Security Culture and the Military in Turkey," *Journal of International Affairs* 54, no. 1 (2000): 199–216, www.jstor .org/stable/24357696; Doğan Akyaz, Nihat Ali Özcan, and Ersel Aydınlı, "The Turkish Military's March toward Europe," *Foreign Affairs* 85, no. 1 (2006): 77–90, www.foreign affairs.com/articles/turkey/2006-01-01/turkish-militarys-march-toward-europe.

6. Bülent Aras, "Reform and Capacity Building in the Turkish Foreign Ministry: Bridging the Gap between Ideas and Institutions," *Journal of Balkan and Near Eastern Studies* 17, no. 3 (2015): 260–85, doi.org/10.1080/19448953.2015.1063271; Şaban Kardaş, "Turkey: A Regional Power Facing a Changing International System," *Turkish Studies* 14, no. 4 (2013): 637–60, doi.org/10.1080/14683849.2013.861111.

7. Interview with a bureaucrat, Ankara, December 21, 2016.

8. Ebru Turhan and Emirhan Yorulmazlar, "Turkish Foreign Policy towards the Arab Spring: Between Western Orientation and Regional Disorder," *Journal of Balkan and Near Eastern Studies* 17, no. 3 (2015): 337–52, doi.org/10.1080/19448953.2015.106 3805.

9. Bülent Aras, *Turkish Foreign Policy after July 15* (İstanbul: Istanbul Policy Center, 2017), 4.

10. Aras, "Reform and Capacity Building."

11. Adalet ve Kalkınma Partisi Programı (Party Program of Justice and Development Party), August 14, 2001, accessed July 8, 2017, www.akparti.org.tr/site/akparti/parti -programi#bolum.

12. Malik Mufti, *Daring and Caution in Turkish Strategic Culture: Republic at Sea* (Basingstoke, UK: Palgrave Macmillan, 2009).

13. Interview with a member of parliament, Ankara, December 21, 2016.

14. Ahmet Davutoğlu, "Turkey's Zero-Problems Foreign Policy," *Foreign Policy*, May 20, 2010, https://foreignpolicy.com/2010/05/20/turkeys-zero-problems-foreign-policy/.

15. Law 2937 on the National Intelligence Organization (MIT) restricted its missions, in principle, to domestic matters. This deficiency at a time when Turkey was heavily involved in Syria engendered political and legal debates about the government and the head of the MIT.

16. Bülent Aras and Zulkarnain Mohammed, "The Turkish Government Scholarship Program as a Soft Power Tool," *Turkish Studies* 20, no. 3 (2018): 421–41, doi.org/10.1 080/14683849.2018.1502042.

17. "Türkiye Dünyada En Çok Dış Temsilciliği Olan 6. Ülke," *TRT Haber* (İstanbul), December 26, 2016, www.trthaber.com/haber/turkiye/turkiye-dunyada-en-cok-dis-temsilciligi-olan-6-ulke-290357.html.

18. Fuat Keyman, "Turkey's Choice: Responding to Security Challenges through Humanitarian Norms with a Revitalized EU Anchor," *International Politics* 54, no. 4 (2017): 453–67, doi.org/10.1057/s41311-017-0042-z.

19. Kareem Fahim and Zakaria, "Turkey Has Deported Hundreds of Syrian Migrants, Advocates and Refugees Say," *Washington Post*, July 22, 2019.

20. Pınar Akpınar, "Turkey's Peacebuilding in Somalia: The Limits of Humanitarian Diplomacy," *Turkish Studies* 14, no. 4 (2013): 735–57, doi.org/10.1080/14683849.2013.863448; Bülent Aras and Pınar Akpınar, "The Role of Humanitarian NGOs in Turkey's Peacebuilding," *International Peacekeeping* 22, no. 3 (2015): 230–47, doi.org/10.1080/13533312.2015.1033374.

21. Tim Arango and Ceylan Yeginsu, "How Erdoğan Moved to Solidify Power by Ousting a Pivotal Ally," *New York Times*, May 5, 2016.

22. Yalçın Akdoğan, *Muhafazakar Demokrasi* (Ankara: AK Parti Yayinları, 2003).

23. Syria became one of the determining elements of Erdoğan's personal relations with foreign leaders, including his US, Russian, and Iranian counterparts. Similar topical issues were also experienced with Israel, Germany, Egypt, Austria, Bangladesh, Iraq, the Gulf monarchies, and Venezuela.

24. Bülent Aras and Richard Falk, "Five Years after the Arab Spring: A Critical Evaluation," *Third World Quarterly* 37, no. 12 (2016): 2252–58, doi.org/10.1080/01436597.2016.1224087.

25. Interview with a member of parliament, Ankara, December 21, 2016.

26. H. L. Smith, "Fahrettin Altun: The Rise and Rise of Turkey's Second Most Powerful Man," *Times* (London), June 18, 2019.

27. Interview with a member of parliament, Ankara, January 4, 2017.

28. "AK Parti'den 7 Ülkede Temsilcilik," *Hurriyet Daily News* (İstanbul), December 29, 2018, www.hurriyetdailynews.com/ruling-akp-plans-to-expand-overseas-with-nine-new-offices-124960.

29. Muhammed Taha Gergerlioğlu, *Türk Tipi Cumhurbaşkanlığı: Kurumların Vesayetinden Halkın İktidarına* (İstanbul: Hayykitap, 2017).

30. Presidential spokesperson Ibrahim Kalın was appointed acting president of the Council. "Kalın'a Yeni Görev," *Habertürk* (İstanbul), November 2, 2018, www.milliyet.com.tr/siyaset/kalin-a-yeni-gorev-2770722.

31. Bülent Aras and Richard Falk, "Who Is the Winner of Turkey's Elections?" *Al Jazeera*, November 16, 2015, www.aljazeera.com/indepth/opinion/2015/11/winner-turkey-elections-151110083204683.html?xif=.

32. Interview with a member of parliament, Ankara, January 4, 2017.

33. Interview with a member of parliament, Ankara, December 21, 2016.

34. An emerging result of the post–15 July political atmosphere has been alienation of the opposition, which later gave way to the Republican People's Party (CHP) leader's 450-kilometer Justice March from Ankara to İstanbul to protest, in particular, the arrest of a CHP member of parliament.

35. "A Russian Propaganda Outlet Prospers in Turkey," *Economist*, February 28, 2019, www.economist.com/europe/2019/02/28/a-russian-propaganda-outlet-prospers-in-turkey.

36. Bulent Aras, "Why Does Turkey Want S-400 Missiles?" *LobeLog*, July 3, 2019, www.lobelog.com/why-does-turkey-want-s-400-missiles/.

37. Şaban Kardaş, "Turkey's S400 vs. F35 Conundrum and Its Deepening Strategic Partnership with Russia," *GMF on Turkey*, May 28, 2019, www.gmfus.org/publications/turkeys-s400-vs-f35-conundrum-and-its-deepening-strategic-partnership-russia; Murat Yetkin, "Türkiye Rusya'ya Bağımlı Hale Getirilmemeli: Kılıçdaroğlu Hükümeti de, ABD'yi de Uyarıyor," *Yetkin Report*, July 23, 2019, https://yetkinreport.com/2019/07/23/turkiye-rusyaya-bagimli-hale-getirilmemeli-kilicdaroglu-hukumeti-de-abdyi-de-uyariyor/.

38. Interview with a member of parliament, Ankara, December 21, 2016.

39. Interview with a bureaucrat, Ankara, December 21, 2016.

40. Davutoğlu later denounced the claims that he was responsible for all foreign policy failures. "Davutoğlu: Erdoğan'ın Benden İsteği 'Başbakan Gibi Görün ama Başbakan Gibi Olma' İdi," *T24* (İstanbul), July 18, 2019, https://t24.com.tr/haber/eski-basbakan-Davutoğlu-canli-yayinda,831151.

41. Murat Yetkin, "PKK Saldırısı, Avrasya Lobisi ve Ürperten Senaryoya Güç Kattı," *Hürriyet* (İstanbul), December 14, 2016, www.hurriyet.com.tr/yazarlar/murat-yetkin/pkk-saldirisi-avrasya-lobisi-ve-urperten-senaryoya-guc-katti-40306102.

42. Aya Samir, "Egypt, Greece, Cyprus: Model for Successful International Cooperation," *Egypt Today*, November 21, 2017, www.egypttoday.com/Article/2/33551/Egypt-Greece-Cyprus-Model-for-successful-international-cooperation.

43. Mehmet Solmaz, "Why Saudi Arabia and the UAE Are Targeting Turkey," *Middle East Eye* (London), December 27, 2017, www.middleeasteye.net/opinion/why-saudi-arabia-and-uae-are-targeting-turkey.

44. Bülent Aras and Emirhan Yorulmazlar, "State, Region, and Order: Geopolitics of the Arab Spring," *Third World Quarterly* 37, no. 12 (2016): 2259–73, doi.org/10.1080/01436597.2016.1205442.

45. Aras and Yorulmazlar, "State."

46. See James Stavridis, "Pushing Turkey out of NATO Is a Terrible Idea," *Bloomberg*, July 18, 2019, www.bloomberg.com/opinion/articles/2019-07-18/kicking-turkey-out-of-nato-would-be-a-gift-to-putin.

47. Aras, *Turkish Foreign Policy*, 12.

48. Aras, *Turkish Foreign Policy*, 12.

5. Reforming Turkey

1. Gizem Karakış, "Yeni Sistemde Revizyon Çalışmaları Başladı," *Hürriyet* (İstanbul), July 13, 2019, www.hurriyet.com.tr/gundem/yeni-sistemde-revizyon-calismalari-basladi-41272592.

2. *Public Sector Reform: What Works and Why? An IEG Evaluation of World Bank Support* (Washington, DC: World Bank, 2018).

3. "Mustafa Yeneroğlu AK Parti'den İstifa Etti," *Hürriyet* (İstanbul), October 30, 2019, www.karar.com/son-dakika-mustafa-yenerolu-ak-partiden-istifa-etti-1368963.

4. Jonathan K. Hanson, "Democracy and State Capacity: Complements or Substitute," *Studies in Comparative International Development* 50, no. 3 (2015): 304–30, https://ssrn.com/abstract=2482403.

5. Cullen S. Hendrix, "Measuring State Capacity: Theoretical and Empirical Implications for the Study of Civil Conflict," *Journal of Peace Research* 47, no. 3 (2010): 273–85, doi.org/10.1177/0022343310361838.

6. Bülent Aras, "Turkey's Future Lies with the West," *LobeLog*, July 25, 2019, https://lobelog.com/turkeys-future-lies-with-the-west/.

7. Chair of the Supreme Court Zuhtu Arslan most recently identified "the protection of fundamental rights" as the state's "common goal, even the raison d'être of the state." See Ali Uludağ, "Yeminlerini Anımsattı," *Cumhuriyet* (İstanbul), July 26, 2019, www.cumhuriyet.com.tr/haber/siyaset/1505444/Yeminlerini_animsatti.html.

8. See "Eski AKP Milletvekili Özdağ'dan Partisine Sert Sözler," *Gazete2023* (İstanbul), February 14, 2019, www.gazete2023.com/siyaset/eski-akp-milletvekili-ozdag-dan-partisine-sert-sozler-h85209.html. See also Abdurrahman Dilipak, "Biz Nerede Yanlış Yaptık!" *Yeni Akit* (İstanbul), April 3, 2019, www.yeniakit.com.tr/yazarlar/abdurrahman-dilipak/biz-nerede-yanlis-yaptik-28034.html.

9. Matthew Hoddie and Caroline Hartzell, "Institutionalizing Peace: Power Sharing and Post–Civil War Conflict Management," *American Journal of Political Science* 47, no. 2 (2003): 330, doi.org/10.1111/1540-5907.00022.

10. Max Weber, *From Max Weber: Essays in Sociology*, trans. and ed. H. H. Gerth and C. Wright Mills (New York: Oxford Univ. Press, 1946).

11. Mohammed Ayoob, "State Making, State Breaking, and State Failure," in *Leashing the Dogs of War: Conflict Management in a Divided World*, ed. Chester Crocker, Fen Hampson, and Pamela Aall, (Washington, DC: United States Institute of Peace, 2007), 95–114.

12. Semra Demir, "An Overview of Peace Education in Turkey: Definitions, Difficulties, and Suggestions: A Qualitative Analysis," *Kuram ve Uygulamada Eğitim Bilimleri* 11 (2011): 1739–45.

13. Interview with a member of parliament, Van, December 7, 2017.

14. Özden Melis Uluğ and J. Christopher Cohrs, "An Exploration of Lay People's Kurdish Conflict Frames in Turkey," *Peace and Conflict: Journal of Peace Psychology* 22, no. 2 (2016): 117, doi.org/10.1037/pac0000165.

15. Interview with a local politician from the People's Democratic Party (HDP), Van, December 6, 2017.

16. Barbara F. Walter, "Building Reputation: Why Governments Fight Some Separatists but Not Others," *American Journal of Political Science* 50, no. 2 (2006): 324, www.jstor.org/stable/3694275.

17. For example, see Alan Yuhas, "So Muslims Beat Columbus to America? They Had Better Get in Line," *Guardian*, November 17, 2014, www.theguardian.com/world/2014/nov/17/muslims-beat-columbus-america-better-get-in-line.

18. A good example has been a retweet by the United Arab Emirates foreign minister about Turkish history, which led to an official response from the presidential spokesperson and the Ministry of Foreign Affairs. See "Turkey Denounces UAE over Divisive 'Propaganda' Retweet," *Al Jazeera*, December 19, 2017, www.aljazeera.com/news/2017/12/turkey-denounces-uae-divisive-propaganda-retweet-171219192504147.html.

Conclusion

1. Bülent Aras, "Opposition in Turkey," *International Policy Digest*, July 20, 2019, https://intpolicydigest.org/2019/07/20/opposition-in-turkey/.

2. "Sistem Çabuk Çöktü: Kabine Revizyonu mu Bekleniyor?," *Cumhuriyet* (İstanbul), March 29, 2019, www.cumhuriyet.com.tr/haber/yerel_yonetimler/1318448/Sistem_cabuk_coktu__Kabine_revizyonu_mu_bekleniyor_.html.

Bibliography

"Abdullah Öcalan'ın 2014 Newroz Mesajı." *Yüksekova Haber*, March 21, 2014. www.yuksekovahaber.com.tr/haber/abdullah-ocalanin-2014-newroz-mesaji-125867.htm.

Acemoğlu, Daron, and James A. Robinson, *Why Nations Fail: The Origins of Power, Prosperity, and Poverty* (New York: Crown, 2012).

Adalet ve Kalkınma Partisi Programı (Party Program of Justice and Development Party), August 14, 2001, accessed July 8, 2017, www.akparti.org.tr/site/akparti/parti-programi#bolum.

"'AK Parti Kapatılmasın' Kararı Çıktı." *Milliyet* (İstanbul), July 30, 2008. www.milliyet.com.tr/siyaset/ak-parti-kapatilmasin-karari-cikti-972729.

"AK Parti'den 7 Ülkede Temsilcilik." *Hürriyet Daily News* (İstanbul), December 29, 2018. www.hurriyetdailynews.com/ruling-akp-plans-to-expand-overseas-with-nine-new-offices-124960.

Akdoğan, Yalçın. *Muhafazakar Demokrasi*. Ankara: AK Parti Yayinları, 2003.

Akkoyunlu, Karabekir, and Kerem Öktem. "Existential Insecurity and the Making of a Weak Authoritarian Regime in Turkey." *Southeast European and Black Sea Studies* 16, no. 4 (2016): 505–27. doi.org/10.1080/14683857.2016.1253225.

Akpınar, Pınar. "Turkey's Peacebuilding in Somalia: The Limits of Humanitarian Diplomacy." *Turkish Studies* 14, no. 4 (2013): 735–57. doi.org/10.1080/14683849.2013.863448.

"AKP'nin Kamuda 'Uyum' Fırsatçılığı." *Cumhuriyet* (İstanbul), October 28, 2017. www.cumhuriyet.com.tr/haber/siyaset/854426/AKP_nin_kamuda__uyum__firsatciligi.htm.

Akyaz, Doğan, Nihat Ali Özcan, and Ersel Aydınlı. "The Turkish Military's March toward Europe." *Foreign Affairs* 85, no. 1 (2006): 77–90. www.foreignaffairs.com/articles/turkey/2006-01-01/turkish-militarys-march-toward-europe.

Altunışık, Meliha Benli. "The Turkish Model and Democratization in the Middle East." *Arab Studies Quarterly* 27, nos. 1/2 (2005): 45–63. www.jstor.org/stable/41859009.

Alyanak, Çiğdem. "Erdoğan'dan Eğitim ve Kültür Özeleştirisi." *Anadolu Ajansı*, February 9, 2017. www.memurlar.net/haber/645272/.

Andersen, David, et al. "State Capacity and Political Regime Stability." *Democratization* 21, no. 7 (2014): 1305–25. doi.org/10.1080/13510347.2014.960204.

Arango, Tim, and Ceylan Yeginsu. "How Erdoğan Moved to Solidify Power by Ousting a Pivotal Ally." *New York Times*, May 5, 2016.

Aras, Bülent. "Opposition in Turkey." *International Policy Digest*, July 20, 2019. https://intpolicydigest.org/2019/07/20/opposition-in-turkey/.

———. "Reform and Capacity Building in the Turkish Foreign Ministry: Bridging the Gap between Ideas and Institutions." *Journal of Balkan and Near Eastern Studies* 17, no. 3 (2015): 260–85. doi.org/10.1080/19448953.2015.1063271.

———. "Turkey's Future Lies with the West." *LobeLog*, July 25, 2019. https://lobelog.com/turkeys-future-lies-with-the-west/.

———. *Turkish Foreign Policy after July 15*. İstanbul: Istanbul Policy Center, 2017.

———. "Why Does Turkey Want S-400 Missiles?" *LobeLog*, July 3, 2019. https://lobelog.com/why-does-turkey-want-s-400-missiles/.

Aras, Bülent, and Pınar Akpınar. "The Role of Humanitarian NGOs in Turkey's Peacebuilding." *International Peacekeeping* 22, no. 3 (2015): 230–47. doi.org/10.1080/13533312.2015.1033374.

Aras, Bülent, and Richard Falk. "Five Years after the Arab Spring: A Critical Evaluation." *Third World Quarterly* 37, no. 12 (2016): 2252–58. doi.org/10.1080/01436597.2016.1224087.

———. "Who Is the Winner of Turkey's Elections?" *Al Jazeera*, November 15, 2015. www.aljazeera.com/indepth/opinion/2015/11/winner-turkey-elections-151110083204683.html?xif.

Aras, Bülent, and Zulkarnain Mohammed. "The Turkish Government Scholarship Program as a Soft Power Tool," *Turkish Studies* 20, no. 3 (2018): 421–41. doi.org/10.1080/14683849.2018.1502042.

Aras, Bülent, and Rabia Karakaya Polat. "From Conflict to Cooperation: Desecuritization of Turkey's Relations with Syria and Iran." *Security Dialogue* 39, no. 5 (2008): 475–95. doi.org/10.1177/0967010608096150.

Aras, Bülent, and Emirhan Yorulmazlar. "State, Region, and Order: Geopolitics of the Arab Spring." *Third World Quarterly* 37, no. 12 (2016): 2259–73. doi.org/10.1080/01436597.2016.1205442.

Ateş, Hazal. "Memurluk Tapulu Mal Değil." *Sabah* (İstanbul), February 21, 2017. www.sabah.com.tr/ekonomi/2017/02/21/memurluk-tapulu-mal-degil.

Aydınlı, Ersel, and Nihat Ali Özcan. "The Conflict Resolution and Counterterrorism Dilemma: Turkey Faces Its Kurdish Question." *Terrorism and Political Violence* 23, no. 3 (2011): 438–57. doi.org/10.1080/09546553.2011.557328.

Ayoob, Mohammed. "State Making, State Breaking, and State Failure." In *Leashing the Dogs of War: Conflict Management in a Divided World*, edited by Chester Crocker, Fen Hampson, and Pamela Aall, 95–114. Washington, DC: United States Institute of Peace, 2007.

Barnett, Michael. "Culture, Strategy, and Foreign Policy Change: Israel's Road to Oslo." *European Journal of International Relations* 5, no. 1 (1999): 5–36. doi.org/10.1177/1354066199005001001.

Başer, Bahar, and Ahmet Erdi Öztürk. *Authoritarian Politics in Turkey: Elections, Resistance, and the AKP*. London: Bloomsbury, 2017.

Biasiori, Lucio, and Giuseppe Marcocci. *Machiavelli, Islam, and the East: Reorienting the Foundations of Modern Political Thought*. Cham, Switzerland: Palgrave Macmillan, 2018.

Bildircin, Mustafa Mert. "FETÖ'den Boşalan Yerler Yeni Tarikatlarla Dolduruldu." *BirGün* (İstanbul), August 11, 2017. www.birgun.net/haber-detay/fetoden-bosalan-yerler-yeni-tarikatlarla-dolduruldu-174268.html.

Brooker, Paul. *Non-Democratic Regimes*. Basingstoke, UK: Palgrave Macmillan, 2014.

"Büyükanıt'ın Konuşmasının Tam Metni." *Hürriyet* (İstanbul), April 12, 2006. www.hurriyet.com.tr/gundem/buyukanitin-konusmasinin-tam-metni-6321761.

Çadırcı, Musa. "Tanzimat'tan Cumhuriyet'e Ülke Yönetimi." In *Tanzimat'tan Cumhuriyet'e Türkiye Ansiklopedisi*, vol. 1, edited by Murat Belge, 214–30. İstanbul: İletişim Yayınları, 1985.

Çağaptay, Soner. *The New Sultan: Erdoğan and the Crisis of Modern Turkey*. London: I. B. Tauris, 2017.

Ceran, Fatih. "From Paradigm Shift to Retooling: The Foundation and Maintenance of the AKP." *Southeast European and Black Sea Studies* 19, no. 1 (2019): 175–93. doi.org/10.1080/14683857.2019.1579858.

Cizre, Ümit. "Demythologyzing the National Security Concept: The Case of Turkey." *Middle East Journal* 57, no. 2 (2003): 213–29.

Cortell, Andrew P., and Susan Peterson. "Limiting the Unintended Consequences of Institutional Change." *Comparative Political Studies* 34, no. 7 (2001): 768–99. doi.org/10.1177/0010414001034007003.

Davutoğlu, Ahmet. "Turkey's Zero-Problems Foreign Policy." *Foreign Policy*, May 20, 2010. https://foreignpolicy.com/2010/05/20/turkeys-zero-problems-foreign-policy/.

"Davutoğlu: Erdoğan'ın Benden İsteği 'Başbakan Gibi Görün ama Başbakan Gibi Olma' İdi." *T24* (İstanbul), July 18, 2019. https://t24.com.tr/haber/eski-basbakan-Davutoğlu-canli-yayinda,831151.

Demir, Semra. "An Overview of Peace Education in Turkey: Definitions, Difficulties, and Suggestions: A Qualitative Analysis." *Kuram ve Uygulamada Eğitim Bilimleri* 11 (2011): 1739–45.

Diamond, Larry. "Facing Up to the Democratic Recession." *Journal of Democracy* 26, no. 1 (2015): 141–55. doi.org/10.1353/jod.2015.0009.

Dilipak, Abdurrahman. "Roller Netleşirken." *Yeni Akit* (İstanbul), November 4, 2017. http://m.yeniakit.com.tr/yazarlar/abdurrahman-dilipak/roller-netlesirken-21700.html.

Dilipak, Abdurrahman. "Biz Nerede Yanlış Yaptık!" *Yeni Akit* (İstanbul), April 3, 2019. www.yeniakit.com.tr/yazarlar/abdurrahman-dilipak/biz-nerede-yanlis yaptik-28034.html.

Dinçer, Ömer. *Türkiye'de Değişim Yapmak Neden Bu Kadar Zor?* İstanbul: Alfa Basım Yayım, 2016.

"Doğu Perinçek'ten Kritik Analiz 'Yargının Altın Devri.'" *Aydınlık* (İstanbul), June 6, 2017. www.aydinlik.com.tr/turkiye/2017-haziran/dogu-perincek-ten-kritik-analiz-yarginin-altin-devri.

Düzel, Neşe. "Interview with Baskın Oran." *Radikal* (İstanbul), June 4, 2007. http://acikradyo.com.tr/arsiv-icerigi/baskin-oranla-soylesi.

Elwood, Sarah. "Beyond Cooptation or Resistance: Urban Spatial Politics, Community Organizations, and GIS-Based Spatial Narratives." *Annals of the Association of American Geographers* 96, no. 2 (2006): 323–41. doi.org/10.1111/j.1467-8306.2006.00480.x.

"Erdoğan: 400 Milletvekili Lazım." *Milliyet* (İstanbul), February 6, 2015. www.milliyet.com.tr/siyaset/erdogan-400-milletvekili-lazim-2009741.

"Erdoğan'ın Diyarbakır Mesajı: Devlet Geçmişte Hatalar Yaptı." *Radikal* (İstanbul), August 13, 2005. www.radikal.com.tr/politika/erdoganin-diyarbakir-mesaji-devlet-gecmiste-hatalar-yapti-754621/.

"Erdoğan's Declaration of 'System Change' Outrages Turkey's Opposition." *Hürriyet Daily News* (İstanbul), August 16, 2015. www.hurriyetdailynews.com/erdogans-declaration-of-system-change-outrages-turkeys-opposition--87036.

Ersoy, Duygu, and Fahriye Üstüner. "'Liberal Intellectuals' Narration of the Justice and Development Party in Turkey." *Turkish Studies* 17, no. 3 (2016): 406–28. doi.org/10.1080/14683849.2016.1166057.

Esen, Berk, and Şebnem Gümüşçü. "Rising Competitive Authoritarianism in Turkey." *Third World Quarterly* 37, no. 9 (2016): 1581–1606. doi.org/10.1080/01436597.2015.1135732.

"Eski AKP Milletvekili Özdağ'dan Partisine Sert Sözler." *Gazete2023* (İstanbul), February 14, 2019. www.gazete2023.com/siyaset/eski-akp-milletvekili-ozdag-dan-partisine-sert-sozler-h85209.html.

Etzioni-Halevy, Eva. *Bureaucracy and Democracy: A Political Dilemma*. London: Routledge & Kegan, 1985.

Fahim, Kareem, and Zakaria Zakaria. "Turkey Has Deported Hundreds of Syrian Migrants, Advocates and Refugees Say." *Washington Post*, July 22, 2019.

"Fethullah Gülen: İsrail'den İzin Almalıydılar." *NTV* (İstanbul), April 6, 2010. www.ntv.com.tr/dunya/fethullah-gulen-israilden-izin-almaliydilar,kIC_HTknIEavwlzh-VOxdg.

Findley, Carter V. *Bureaucratic Reform in the Ottoman Empire: The Sublime Porte, 1789–1922*. Princeton, NJ: Princeton Univ. Press, 1980.

Fukuyama, Francis. *State-Building: Governance and World Order in the 21st Century*. Ithaca, NY: Cornell Univ. Press, 2004.

Gergerlioğlu, Muhammed Taha. *Türk Tipi Cumhurbaşkanlığı: Kurumların Vesayetinden Halkın İktidarına*. İstanbul: Hayykitap, 2017.

Gökçe, Gökhan. "Interview with Özlem Zengin." *TRT Haber* (İstanbul), February 15, 2017. www.youtube.com/watch?v=yGSqpQy7T4o.

Gunter, Michael M. "Erdogan and the Decline of Turkey." *Middle East Policy* 23, no. 4 (2016): 123–35. doi.org/10.1111/mepo.12238.

Hanson, Jonathan K. "Democracy and State Capacity: Complements or Substitutes?" *Studies in Comparative International Development* 50, no. 3 (2015): 304–30. https://ssrn.com/abstract=2482403.

Hay, Colin. "Narrating Crisis: The Discursive Construction of the 'Winter of Discontent.'" *Sociology* 30, no. 2 (1996): 253–77. doi.org/10.1177/0038038596030002004.

Hendrix, Cullen S. "Measuring State Capacity: Theoretical and Empirical Implications for the Study of Civil Conflict." *Journal of Peace Research* 47, no. 3 (2010): 273–85. doi.org/10.1177/0022343310361838.

Heper, Metin. *The State Tradition in Turkey*. Beverley, UK: Eothen, 1985.

Heper, Metin. "The Strong State as a Problem for the Consolidation of Democracy: Turkey and Germany Compared." *Comparative Political Studies* 25, no. 2 (1992): 169–94. doi.org/10.1177/0010414092025002002.

Heper, Metin. "The Ottoman Legacy and Turkish Politics." *Journal of International Affairs* 54, no. 1 (2000): 63–82. www.jstor.org/stable/24357689.

Heper, Metin, and E. Fuat Keyman. "Double-Faced State: Political Patronage and the Consolidation of Democracy in Turkey." *Middle Eastern Studies* 34, no. 4 (1998): 259–77. doi.org/10.1080/00263209808701251.

Hermann, Charles F. "Changing Course: When Governments Choose to Redirect Foreign Policy." *International Studies Quarterly* 34, no. 1 (1990): 3–21. doi.org/10.2307/2600403.

Heydemann, Steven, and Reinoud Leenders. "Authoritarian Learning and Authoritarian Resilience: Regime Responses to the 'Arab Awakening.'" *Globalizations* 8, no. 5 (2011): 647–53. doi.org/10.1080/14747731.2011.621274.

Hoddie, Matthew, and Caroline Hartzell. "Institutionalizing Peace: Power Sharing and Post–Civil War Conflict Management." *American Journal of Political Science* 47, no. 2 (2003): 318–32. doi.org/10.1111/1540-5907.00022.

Hoehne, Markus V. "Limits of Hybrid Political Orders: The Case of Somaliland." *Journal of Eastern African Studies* 7, no. 2 (2013): 199–217. doi.org/10.1080/17531055.2013.776279.

Holsti, Kalevi J. *The State, War, and the State of War*. Cambridge, UK: Cambridge Univ. Press, 2004.

Huntington, Samuel P. *The Third Wave: Democratization in the Late Twentieth Century*. Norman: Univ. of Oklahoma Press, 1991.

İnalcık, Halil. *Osmanlı'da Devlet, Hukuk Ve Adâlet*. İstanbul: Kronik, 2016.

Kalaycıoğlu, Ersin. "The Conundrum of Coalition Politics in Turkey." *Turkish Studies* 17, no. 1 (2016): 31-38. doi.org/10.1080/14683849.2015.1136087.

"Kalın'a Yeni Görev." *Habertürk* (İstanbul), November 2, 2018. www.milliyet.com.tr/siyaset/kalin-a-yeni-gorev-2770722.

Karaer, Tacettin. "12 Eylül ve Türk Kamu Yönetiminin Yeniden Düzenlenmesi." *Amme İdaresi Dergisi* 20, no. 3 (1987): 29–54.

Karakış, Gizem. "Yeni Sistemde Revizyon Çalışmaları Başladı." *Hürriyet* (İstanbul), July 13, 2019. www.hurriyet.com.tr/gundem/yeni-sistemde-revizyon-calismalari-basladi-41272592.

Karaosmanoğlu, Ali L. "The Evolution of the National Security Culture and the Military in Turkey." *Journal of International Affairs* 54, no. 1 (2000): 199–216. www.jstor.org/stable/24357696.

Kardaş, Şaban. "The Domestic-Regional Nexus in Turkey's Counterterrorism." *GMF on Turkey*, January 8, 2019. www.gmfus.org/publications/domestic-regional-nexus-turkeys-counterterrorism-policy.

———. "Turkey: A Regional Power Facing a Changing International System." *Turkish Studies* 14, no. 4 (2013): 637–60. doi.org/10.1080/14683849.2013.861111.

———. "Turkey's S400 vs. F35 Conundrum and Its Deepening Strategic Partnership with Russia." *GMF on Turkey*, May 28, 2019. www.gmfus.org/publications/turkeys-s400-vs-f35-conundrum-and-its-deepening-strategic-partnership-russia.

Kentel, Ferhat, and Gevorg Poghosyan. *Ermenistan ve Türkiye Vatandaşları Karşılıklı Algılama ve Diyalog Projesi*. İstanbul: TESEV, 2005.

Keyman, Fuat. "Turkey's Choice: Responding to Security Challenges through Humanitarian Norms with a Revitalized EU Anchor." *International Politics* 54, no. 4 (2017): 453–67. doi.org/10.1057/s41311-017-0042-z.

Kılıçdaroğlu, Kemal. "Tek Adam Değil, Parlamenter Sistem İstiyoruz." *CNN TÜRK* (İstanbul), July 9, 2017. www.cnnturk.com/video/turkiye/kilicdaroglu-tek-adam-degil-parlamenter-sistem-istiyoruz.

"Kurdish Solution Process Will Continue: Turkish PM." *Anadolu Agency*, March 14, 2014. www.aa.com.tr/en/turkey/kurdish-solution-process-will-continue-turkish-pm/174736.

Lindvall, Johannes. *Reform Capacity*. Oxford, UK: Oxford Univ. Press, 2017.

Lindvall, Johannes, and Jan Teorell. "State Capacity as Power: A Conceptual Framework." *STANCE Working Paper Series* 1 (2016): 1–18. https://portal.research.lu.se/portal/en/publications/state-capacity-as-power-a-conceptual-framework(ca52e85b-f17e-401d-9414-c5f52ec860e9).html#Overview.

Mangla, Akshay. "Bureaucratic Norms and State Capacity in India: Implementing Primary Education in the Himalayan Region." *Asian Survey* 55, no. 5 (2015): 882–908. doi.org/10.1525/as.2015.55.5.882.

Mann, Michael. "The Autonomous Power of the State: Its Origins, Mechanisms, and Results." *European Journal of Sociology / Archives Européennes De Sociologie* 25, no. 2 (1984): 185–213. doi.org/10.1017/S0003975600004239.

Mardin, Şerif. "Center-Periphery Relations: A Key to Turkish Politics?." *Daedalus* 102, no. 1 (1973): 169–90. www.jstor.org/stable/i20024104.

Masters, James, and Becky Anderson. "Erdogan Insists Turkey Reforms Don't Make Him a Dictator." *CNN International*, April 18, 2017. www.cnn.com/2017/04/18/europe/erdogan-turkey-interview/index.html.

Migdalovitz, Carol. *Turkey's 2007 Elections: Crisis of Identity and Power.* Washington, DC: Congressional Research Service, 2007.

Mohamad Shukri, Syaza Farhana, and Ishtiaq Hossain. "Strategic Shifts in Discourse by the AKP in Turkey, 2002–2015." *Mediterranean Quarterly* 28, no. 3 (2017): 5–26. doi.org/10.1215/10474552-4216388.

Moon, Bruce E., and William J. Dixon. "Politics, the State, and Basic Human Needs: A Cross-National Study." *American Journal of Political Science* 29, no. 4 (1985): 661–94. www.jstor.org/stable/2111176.

Mufti, Malik. *Daring and Caution in Turkish Strategic Culture: Republic at Sea.* Basingstoke, UK: Palgrave Macmillan, 2009.

"Mustafa Yeneroğlu AK Parti'den İstifa Etti." *Hürriyet* (İstanbul), October 30, 2019. www.karar.com/son-dakika-mustafa-yenerolu-ak-partiden-istifa-etti-1368963.

Nasr, Vali. *The Rise of Islamic Capitalism: Why the New Muslim Middle Class Is the Key to Defeating Extremism.* New York: Free Press, 2010.

Öneş, Cevat. "Güvenlik ve Demokrasi." *Radikal* (İstanbul), December 28, 2005.

Özbudun, Ergun. "Turkey's Judiciary and the Drift toward Competitive Authoritarianism." *International Spectator* 50, no. 2 (2015): 42–45. doi.org/10.1080/03932729.2015.1020651.

Özcan, Ali Kemal. *Turkey's Kurds in Perspective: A Theoretical Analysis of Abdullah Öcalan and the PKK.* London: Routledge, 2006.

Özpek, Burak Bilgehan. "The State's Changing Role regarding the Kurdish Question of Turkey: From Consistent Tutelage to Volatile Securitization." *Alternatives: Global, Local, Political* 44, no. 1 (2019): 35–49. doi.org/10.1177/0304375419854599.

Öztürk, Ahmet Erdi. "An Alternative Reading of Religion and Authoritarianism: The New Logic between Religion and State in the AKP's New Turkey." *Southeast European and Black Sea Studies* 19, no. 1 (2019): 79–98. doi.org/10.1080/14683857.2019.1576370.

Polat, Necati. *Regime Change in Contemporary Turkey: Politics, Rights, Mimesis.* Edinburgh, Scotland: Edinburgh Univ. Press, 2016.

Pope, Nicole. "Turkey: Marching toward One-Man Rule." *Journal of International Affairs* 71, no. 1 (2017): 17–30. www.jstor.org/stable/26494361.

"A Russian Propaganda Outlet Prospers in Turkey." *Economist*, February 28, 2019. www.economist.com/europe/2019/02/28/a-russian-propaganda-outlet-prospers-in-turkey.

Samir, Aya. "Egypt, Greece, Cyprus: Model for Successful International Cooperation." *Egypt Today*, November 21, 2017. www.egypttoday.com/Article/2/33551/Egypt-Greece-Cyprus-Model-for-successful-international-cooperation.

Selçuk, Orçun. "Strong Presidents and Weak Institutions: Populism in Turkey, Venezuela, and Ecuador." *Southeast European and Black Sea Studies* 16, no. 4 (2016): 571–89. doi.org/10.1080/14683857.2016.1242893.

"Sistem Çabuk Çöktü: Kabine Revizyonu mu Bekleniyor?" *Cumhuriyet* (İstanbul), March 29, 2019. www.cumhuriyet.com.tr/haber/yerel_yonetimler/1318448/Sistem_cabuk_coktu__Kabine_revizyonu_mu_bekleniyor_.html.

Slater, Dan, and Sofia Fenner. "State Power and Staying Power: Infrastructural Mechanisms and Authoritarian Durability." *Journal of International Affairs* 65, no. 1 (2011): 15–29. www.jstor.org/stable/24388179.

Smith, H. L. "Fahrettin Altun: The Rise and Rise of Turkey's Second Most Powerful Man." *Times* (London), June 18, 2019.

Solmaz, Mehmet. "Why Saudi Arabia and the UAE Are Targeting Turkey." *Middle East Eye* (London), December 27, 2017. www.middleeasteye.net/opinion/why-saudi-arabia-and-uae-are-targeting-turkey.

Sözen, Süleyman. "New Public Administration in Turkey," in *Turkey's Democratization Process*, edited by Carmen Rodríguez et al., 223–40. London: Routledge, 2014.

Stavridis, James. "Pushing Turkey out of NATO Is a Terrible Idea." *Bloomberg*, July 18, 2019. www.bloomberg.com/opinion/articles/2019-07-18/kicking-turkey-out-of-nato-would-be-a-gift-to-putin.

Suissa, Rachel. "Conflict as a Learning Process: States Conflict versus State and Non-State Actor Conflict." *Defence Studies* 11, no. 2 (2011): 323–45. doi.org/10.1080/14702436.2011.590395.

Taş, Hakkı. "A History of Turkey's AKP-Gülen Conflict." *Mediterranean Politics* 23, no. 3 (2018): 395–402. doi.org/10.1080/13629395.2017.1328766.

Tendler, Judith. *Good Government in the Tropics.* Baltimore, MD: Johns Hopkins Univ. Press, 1998.

"Terörün Toplam Maliyetini Açıkladı." *Milliyet* (İstanbul), October 26, 2013. www.milliyet.com.tr/ekonomi/terorun-toplam-maliyetini-acikladi-1782715.

"Toplumsal Barış Yollarının Araştırılması ve Çözüm Sürecinin Değerlendirilmesi Amaciyla Kurulan Meclis Araştırma Komisyonu Raporu" (Report of Parliament's Steering Committee for Inquiry of the Societal Peace and Resolution Process), http://tbmm.gov.tr/komisyon/cozum_sureci/docs/cozum_kom_raporu.pdf.

Turan, Osman. "The Ideal of World Domination among the Medieval Turks." *Studia Islamica*, no. 4 (1995): 77–90. doi.org/10.2307/1595052.

Turhan, Ebru, and Emirhan Yorulmazlar. "Turkish Foreign Policy towards the Arab Spring: Between Western Orientation and Regional Disorder." *Journal of Balkan and Near Eastern Studies* 17, no. 3 (2015): 337–52. doi.org/10.1080/19448953.2015.1063805.

"Turk Halkina Atılan Tekme." *Deutsche Welle* (Ankara), May 16, 2014. www.dw.com/tr/türk-halkına-atılan-tekme/a-17640185.

"Turkey Denounces UAE over Divisive 'Propaganda' Retweet." *Al Jazeera*, December 19, 2017. www.aljazeera.com/news/2017/12/turkey-denounces-uae-divisive-propaganda-retweet-171219192504147.html.

"Turkey Locks Up Dissidents." *Economist*, November 10, 2016. www.economist.com/europe/2016/11/10/turkey-locks-up-dissidents.

"Türkiye Dünyada En Çok Dış Temsilciliği Olan 6. Ülke." *TRT Haber* (İstanbul), December 26, 2016. www.trthaber.com/haber/turkiye/turkiye-dunyada-en-cok-dis-temsilciligi-olan-6-ulke-290357.html.

Turkut, Emre. "Accommodating Security Imperatives v. Protecting Fundamental Rights: The Challenge of States of Emergency in the Context of Countering Terrorism in Turkey." *Security and Human Rights* 28 (2019): 62–91. doi.org/10.1163/18750230-02801002.

TÜSİAD, *Türk Demokrasisi'nde 130 Yıl (1876–2006): Prof. Bülent Tanör'ün Anısına Türkiye'de Demokratikleşme Perspektifleri 10. Yıl Güncellemesi*. Report no. TÜSIAD-T/2006-12/426 (İstanbul: TÜSIAD, 2006). https://tusiad.org/tr/yayinlar/raporlar/item/5290-turk-demokrasisinde-130-yil-1876-2006.

Uludağ, Ali. "Yeminlerini Anımsattı." *Cumhuriyet* (İstanbul), July 26, 2019. www.cumhuriyet.com.tr/haber/siyaset/1505444/Yeminlerini_animsatti.html.

Uluengin, Hadi. "Arınç'ın Manifestosu." *Hürriyet* (İstanbul), April 25, 2006. www.hurriyet.com.tr/arinc-in-manifestosu-4309821.

Uluğ, Özden Melis, and J. Christopher Cohrs. "An Exploration of Lay People's Kurdish Conflict Frames in Turkey." *Peace and Conflict: Journal of Peace Psychology* 22, no. 2 (2016): 109–19. doi.org/10.1037/pac0000165.

Walter, Barbara F. "Building Reputation: Why Governments Fight Some Separatists but Not Others." *American Journal of Political Science* 50, no. 2 (2006): 313–30. www.jstor.org/stable/3694275.

Weber, Max. *From Max Weber: Essays in Sociology*. Translated and edited by H. H. Gerth and C. Wright Mills. New York: Oxford Univ. Press, 1946.

White, Jenny. "Spindle Autocracy in the New Turkey." *Brown Journal of World Affairs* 24, no. 1 (2017): 23–37. http://bjwa.brown.edu/24-1/spindle-autocracy-in-the-new-turkey/.

Widmaier, Wesley W., Mark Blyth, and Leonard Seabrooke. "Exogenous Shocks or Endogenous Constructions?: The Meanings of Wars and Crises." *International Studies Quarterly* 51, no. 4 (2007): 747–59. doi.org/10.1111/j.1468-2478.2007.00474.x.

Wilson, James Q. *Bureaucracy: What Government Agencies Do and Why They Do It*. New York: Basic Books, 2001.

World Bank. *Public Sector Reform: What Works and Why? An IEG Evaluation of World Bank Support*. Washington, DC: World Bank, 2018.

Yavuz, M. Hakan. "Understanding Turkish Secularism in the 21th Century: A Contextual Roadmap." *Southeast European and Black Sea Studies* 19, no. 1 (2019): 55–78. doi.org/10.1080/14683857.2019.1576367.

Yavuz, M. Hakan, and Nihat Ali Özcan. "Turkish Democracy and the Kurdish Question," *Middle East Policy* 24, no. 4 (2015): 73–87. doi.org/10.1111/mepo.12159.

Yeğen, Mesut. "The Kurdish Peace Process in Turkey: Genesis, Evolution, and Prospects." Global Turkey in Europe Working Paper no. 11 (2015): 1–15. www.iai.it/sites/default/files/gte_wp_11.pdf.

Yetkin, Murat. "PKK Saldırısı, Avrasya Lobisi ve Ürperten Senaryoya Güç Kattı." *Hürriyet* (İstanbul), December 14, 2016. www.hurriyet.com.tr/yazarlar/murat-yetkin/pkk-saldirisi-avrasya-lobisi-ve-urperten-senaryoya-guc-katti-40306102.

Yetkin, Murat. "Türkiye Rusya'ya Bağımlı Hale Getirilmemeli: Kılıçdaroğlu Hükümeti de, ABD'yi de Uyarıyor." *Yetkin Report*, July 23, 2019. https://yetkinreport.com/2019/07/23/turkiye-rusyaya-bagimli-hale-getirilmemeli-kilicdaroglu-hukumeti-de-abdyi-de-uyariyor/.

Yılmaz, Muharrem. "'Çözüme Yatırım' ve Bölgesel Kalkınma." *TÜSİAD Görüş Dergisi*, (2013): 13–18. https://tusiad.org/tr/tum/item/6861-tusiad-yonetim-kurulu-baskani-muharrem-yilmazin-gorus-dergisinin-temmuz-2013-sayisinda-yayinlanan-cozume-yatirim-ve-bolgesel-kalkinma-baslikli-makalesi.

Yılmaz, Zafer. "The AKP and the Spirit of the 'New' Turkey: Imagined Victim, Reactionary Mood, and Resentful Sovereign." *Turkish Studies* 18, no. 3 (2017): 482–513. doi.org/10.1080/14683849.2017.1314763.

Yinanç, Barçın. "Ample Evidence to Prove that Gülenists Were behind Turkey's Coup Attempt: Journalist Sedat Ergin." *Hurriyet Daily News* (İstanbul), August 28, 2017. www.hurriyetdailynews.com/ample-evidence-to-prove-that-gulenists-were-behind-turkeys-coup-attempt-journalist-sedat-ergin-117241.

———. "Gülenists 'Abused' Efforts to Enhance Democracy: Ruling AKP Official." *Hurriyet Daily News* (İstanbul), July 17, 2017. www.hurriyetdailynews.com/gulenists-abused-efforts-to-enhance-democracy-ruling-akp-official-115570.

Yörük, Erdem. "The Long Summer of Turkey: The Gezi Uprising and Its Historical Roots." *South Atlantic Quarterly* 113, no. 2 (2014): 419–26. doi.org/10.1215/00382876-2644203.

Yuhas, Alan. "So Muslims Beat Columbus to America? They Had Better Get in Line." *Guardian*, November 17, 2014. www.theguardian.com/world/2014/nov/17/muslims-beat-columbus-america-better-get-in-line.

Index

Italic page numbers denote tables.

Bülent Aras is senior scholar and coordinator of the Conflict Resolution and Mediation Stream at Istanbul Policy Center, visiting professor at the Gulf Research Center at Qatar University, and research professor of international relations at Rensselaer Polytechnic Institute. He was the academic advisor to Ahmet Davutoğlu, then minister of foreign affairs of the Republic of Turkey, from 2009 to 2014. Before joining IPC, Aras worked at Turkey's Ministry of Foreign Affairs as chair at the Center for Strategic Research and the Diplomatic Academy between 2010 and 2013. He also taught in the Department of Humanities and Social Sciences at Istanbul Technical University. In 2010 he was senior visiting professor of Turkish studies at St. Antony's College, Oxford. He was a research scholar at the Paris-based European Union Institute of Security Studies in the summer of 2004, at Oxford University's St. Antony's College in 2003, and at Indiana University's Center for Eurasian Studies in 1998. His writings include *Palestinian-Israeli Peace Process and Turkey* (Nova Science, 1998), *New Geopolitics of Eurasia and Turkey's Position* (Frank Cass, 2002), and, as coeditor, *Turkey, the Arab Spring, and Beyond* (Routledge, 2016) and *Oil and Geopolitics in the Caspian Sea Region* (Praeger, 1999). His articles have appeared in numerous academic journals, magazines, and newspapers and have been translated into several languages, including Persian, Russian, and Arabic. Aras received his PhD in international relations from Boğaziçi University in 1999.